A Practical Guide to the Law of Parking in Great Britain

A Practical Guide to the Law of Parking in Great Britain

Iain G. Mitchell KC

Advocate, Scotland

Barrister, Middle Temple

LLB (Hons); FRSA; Fellow, European Law Institute

Law Brief Publishing

© Iain G. Mitchell

All rights reserved. No part of this publication may be reproduced, stored in a retrieval system, or transmitted, in any form or by any means, electronic, mechanical, photocopying, recording or otherwise, without the prior permission of the publisher.

Excerpts from judgments and statutes are Crown copyright. Any Crown Copyright material is reproduced with the permission of the Controller of OPSI and the King's Printer for Scotland. Some quotations may be licensed under the terms of the Open Government Licence (http://www.nationalarchives.gov.uk/doc/open-government-licence/version/3).

Cover image © iStockphoto.com/Tisomboon

The information in this book was believed to be correct at the time of writing. All content is for information purposes only and is not intended as legal advice. No liability is accepted by either the publisher or author for any errors or omissions (whether negligent or not) that it may contain. Professional advice should always be obtained before applying any information to particular circumstances.

Published 2024 by Law Brief Publishing, an imprint of Law Brief Publishing Ltd
30 The Parks
Minehead
Somerset
TA24 8BT

www.lawbriefpublishing.com

Paperback: 978-1-916698-48-2

Among its many charms Huron County boasts magnificent sunsets. If you look west from the plaintiffs' right of way along the lake bluff on a summer's evening the spectacle of the fiery orb sinking into the inland sea is sure to instil a sense of calm tranquillity. That feeling is an illusion! The very ground beneath your feet convulses in contending claims of adverse possession, prescriptive easement, and proprietary estoppel. It is a privilege of the people to enjoy sunsets but the lot of lawyers to litigate land disputes.

– Donohue J in *Lafferty and anr v Brindley*, Ontario Supreme Court, 25 July 2001, unreported, quoted by Lord Marnoch in *Moncrieff v Jamieson* 2005 1SC 281 at 283, paragraph [1].

PREFACE

Apart perhaps from boundary disputes, few areas of land law generate as much heat, and cause litigants to act as irrationally as parking.

There is a certain note of exasperation in the comments of Lady Justice Arden in the court of Appeal in *Waterman v Boyle* [2009] EWCA Civ 116 at paragraphs [39] and [40]:

"There is a common misunderstanding that an Englishman's home is his castle in the sense that he can build walls, put up gates and do other acts on his land whenever he chooses, and without regard for his neighbours. In this case, Mr Boyle and Ms Gwilt, in an effort to stop parking on the northern drive, had even engaged a clamping firm and put up warning notices about the risk of clamping (which never in fact occurred). In related proceedings brought by the Watermans against their solicitors, in which Mr Boyle gave evidence, HHJ Dean QC had described such a step between close neighbours as verging 'on the edge of rationality'.

> "While it is often true that a person can do what he wants on his own land, it is not always so. The law expects neighbours to show some give and take towards each other. The parties to this litigation should keep that point in mind for the future and now draw a line under the past. Parties to other boundary disputes and their advisers should also, at all times, have this point firmly at the forefront of their minds, and seek to resolve their disputes accordingly, and without resort to complex and expensive litigation."

Similarly, in *Moncrieff v Jamieson* 2008 SC (HL) 1, Lord Hope of Craighead (at paragraph [19]) and Lord Neuberger of Abbotsbury (at paragraph [105]) described that case as "unfortunate". Lord Scott was more direct at paragraph [45] when he said:

> "This case is also a very sad one for it evidences a regrettable and surely unnecessary falling out between neighbours who had lived as neighbours in apparent amity for very many years, sorting out questions of mutual concern regarding the respondents' access to their property, Da Store, by sensible arrangements without recourse to the law. The problems that have led to the falling out, to the commencement and conduct of expensive litigation and to their presence now before your Lordships as litigants relate to the right of way over the appellants' land to which the respondents are entitled in order to obtain access to Da Store from the Sandsound public road. The respondents' right of way, the existence of which has never been in dispute, has, over the years since 1973 when the right was first granted, required arrangements to be settled regarding the manner of its exercise. These are matters that neighbours, having due regard for one another's reasonable requirements and interests, ought to be able to sort out for themselves. But if, for whatever reason, they cannot or do not do so, the law must do so for them and, where the exercise of servitudes, or easements, is in question, will do so by reference to those reasonable requirements and interests."

Lord Roger of Earlsferry was having none of it.

He said (at paragraph [66])

> "Your Lordships have variously described it as an 'unfortunate case', as a 'sad one' and as an 'unfortunate matter'. The parties are, however, adults and the dispute between them is genuine. Since the point at issue is difficult, it is not surprising that they have been unable to resolve it for themselves. In these circumstances they have simply chosen to exercise their right to have it resolved by the courts. Those on one side have decided to spend their own money

on doing so; the Legal Aid Board has financed the other side. As a judge, I would not describe the resulting situation as sad or unfortunate: after all, courts exist and judges are paid to resolve such disputes, which are indeed the life blood of the common law."

It is the modest purpose of this book to give some measure of guidance to practitioners and would-be litigants in both Scotland and England & Wales which might, perhaps, lead to the resolution of their disputes without resort to the sort of complex and expensive litigation on which Lord Roger looks with such equanimity.

In presenting this book, I should like to thank my editor at Law Brief Publishing and friends and colleagues, including Lewis Walker and Ali Kazmi, Barrister-at-law, who have read the text and provided helpful suggestions and revisions. However, should there be any errors remaining they are down to me and not to them.

The law is stated as at 31st July, 2024.

Iain G. Mitchell KC
Arnot Manderson Advocates, Edinburgh
Tanfield Chambers, London
August 2024

CONTENTS

Chapter One	Public Parking	1
Chapter Two	Private Car Parks	25
Chapter Three	Private Parking Rights: The Servitude of Parking	43
Chapter Four	Servitudes and Real Burdens in Scotland in Terms of the Title Conditions (Scotland) Act 2003	79
Chapter Five	Parking Under Leases and Other Rights	83
Chapter Six	The Exercise of the Private Parking Rights	85
Chapter Seven	Afterword	95

CHAPTER ONE

PUBLIC PARKING

Introduction

Different legal regimes may apply to car parking, depending upon whether it takes place on-street or off street. Where the parking is on-street, the rules differ as to whether the road in question is a highway or road (as defined in legislation) or not, and, if a public street, whether or not it is subject to an Order controlling parking.

Where parking takes place in an off-street car park, again, different legal regimes apply depending on whether the car park is provided by a local authority or a private actor.

Parking on Roads and Highways

Classification of Roads:

In England and Wales, a "highway" is defined by section 328 of the Highways Act 1980, which states:

> "(1) In this Act, except where the context otherwise requires, "highway" means the whole or a part of a highway other than a ferry or waterway…"

There is a circularity in that definition as it says what a highway includes, rather than what it is. However, the characteristics of what makes a road a highway can be found in case law. These are as follows.

First, highways are not restricted as to the persons who may use them – they must be open to use by the public as a whole. Further, that public use must be as of right. For example, in *Kotegaonkar v Secretary of State for the Environment, Food and Rural Affairs* [2012] EWHC 1976 (Admin), the court found that a route of paving stones linking a health centre with a parade of shops could not be a highway as it could be reached at each end only through private property, access to which could be given only by permission of the respective owners.

Second, the right is essentially one of passage (*Goodtitle, ex dimiss. Chester v Alker and Elmes* (1757) 97 ER 231), although it was recognised in *D.P.P v Jones* [1999] 2 A.C. 240 that members of the public can use a highway for any reasonable purpose so long as their activities are otherwise lawful and do not obstruct the right of passage for other members of the public.

Third, a highway is any way over which there is a public right of way. Thus, it encompasses both public roads and private roads which are subject to a public right of way. In this respect, it is not dissimilar to a servitude right of access. (See Lord Hope of Craighead in *DPP v Jones* at page 268H)

In Scotland, at common law, the position is substantially similar.

In *Waddell v The Earl of Buchan* (1868) 6 M 690 at page 699, Lord Curriehill states that:

> "A right of Highway confers on the public a right to use the surface for the ordinary purposes of locomotion. It is a kind of right that has existed in this country and elsewhere from the infancy of civilisation... The nature of the right is a right to use the surface for the purpose of locomotion by carriage or on foot, but not to exercise any other rights of property."

In Ferguson, *The Law of Roads, Streets, and Rights of Way, Bridges and Ferries in Scotland* (1904) it is said at page 4:

> "A highway is a right of passage to all the king's subjects

without distinction"

Rankine, *The Law of Land-ownership in Scotland,* 4th edn. (1909) states at page 325 that the definition of a highway in English law as "a right of passage in general to all the King's subjects" applies also to Scotland, and, as in England, a right of highway may be exercised also over a private road. In *Wills' Trustees v. Cairngorm Canoeing and Sailing School Ltd.,* 1976 S.C. (H.L.) 30, at page 125 Lord Wilberforce said: "A public right of way on highways is established by use over the land of a proprietor . . ." (see also Lord Hope of Craighead in *DPP v Jones* at page 269F).

This clarity was clouded somewhat by the statutory definition of a Highway in section 1 of the *Roads and Bridges (Scotland) Act 1878:*

> "Highway" shall mean and include all existing turnpike roads, all existing statute labour roads, all roads maintained under the provisions of the Highland Roads and Bridges Act 1862, and all bridges forming part of any highway, and all other roads when declared when declared to be highways under the provisions of this Act, all public streets and roads within any burgh or police burgh not at the commencement of this Act vested in the local authority thereof, but shall not include any street or road so vested, or any street or road or bridge which any person is at the commencement of this Act bound to maintain at his own expense."

It will be noted that this statutory definition is not restricted to saying what is included in the definition, but also what the definition "shall mean", and the notable exclusion from the statutory definition is "any street or road or bridge which any person is at the commencement of this Act bound to maintain at his own expense",

which would exclude private roads from the statutory provisions for the purposes of the 1878 Act.

There were other statutory provisions containing statutory definitions of "roads" referring also to highways. In particular, section 104 (1) of the *Road Traffic Regulation Act 1967* contained the definition:

> "'road' means any highway and any other road to which the public has access..."

The 1967 Act was repealed by the *Road Traffic Regulation Act 1984*, which carried over the above definition into section 142(1) of that Act.

This was followed shortly afterwards by section 151 of the *Roads (Scotland) Act 1984* which contains the following definitions:

> "'Road' means, subject to subsection (3) below, any way (other than a waterway) over which there is a public right of passage (by whatever means and whether subject to a toll or not) and includes the road's verge, and any bridge (whether permanent or temporary) over which, or tunnel through which, the road passes; and any reference to a road includes a part thereof;
>
> "private road" means any road other than a public road;
>
> "public road" means a road which a roads authority have a duty to maintain;".

Furthermore paragraph 93(44)(d) of Schedule 10 of the *Roads (Scotland) Act 1984*, amended the definition in section 142(1) of *Road Traffic Regulations Act 1984* (very shortly after its original enactment) to bring it into line with the definition given in the *Roads (Scotland) Act 1984*. By those means, the word "highway" disappeared from the statutory classification of roads in Scotland.

This is not a mere terminological change, but represents a conscious restatement of the law. This is explained by the Inner House of the Court of Session in *Hamilton v Dumfries and Galloway Council* (No 2) 2009 SC 277 at paragraph [25]:

> "The 1984 Act rationalised Scottish legislation relating to roads, which was previously to be found in a large number of statutes of varying application: some, for example, were of local application, others applied only to the former burghs, and others again applied only to roads in the countryside. It was a codifying rather than consolidating measure: it introduced innovations as well as bringing provisions together in a single statute. In particular, it employed the term 'road', as defined in the Act, in place of the various terms (such as 'highway', 'street', 'road' and 'carriageway'), variously defined, which were employed in earlier legislation."

If one reads across from the concept of "Highway" to the statutory language of section 151 of the *Roads (Scotland) Act 1984*, there is a commonality – the existence of a public right of passage – between a highway and a "road" as defined. However, the Scottish classification does not map perfectly on to the English terminology.

This is apparent from paragraph [27] of *Hamilton*:

> It is important to note that the distinction between the expressions 'public road' and 'private road', as those expressions are used in the 1984 Act, has nothing to do with the existence of a public right of passage: public roads and private roads, as defined, are all alike ways over which there is a public right of passage. The distinction relates solely to the question whether the roads authority have a duty to maintain the road in question. A 'private road' within the meaning of the Act is therefore entirely different from what, in ordinary language, would usually be described as a private road: that is to say, a road over which the public have no right of passage. In the language of the Act, such a road is not a 'private road': it is not a 'road' of any kind."

The net result is that some roads which are private are "private roads" as defined in section 151 if there is a public right of passage over them, whereas other self-evidently private roads are not roads at all.

This distinction between the Scottish and English categorisations needs is reflected in provisions such as section 34 (1)(a) of the Rpad Traffic Regulations Act 1984:

> "(1) Where it appears to a local authority. . .which proposes to provide, or has provided, an off-street parking place under section 32 of this Act -
>
> (a) that it would relieve or prevent congestion of traffic on *a highway or, in Scotland, a road* if use were made of the parking place to provide a means of access from the *highway or road* to premises adjoining, or abutting on, the parking place..." [*Emphasis supplied*]."

Therefore, when looking at issues concerning roads in Scotland, it is important to bear the difference in categorisation in mind. However, when considering the issue of parking, the important question is simply whether there is a public right of passage. If there is, that would lead in England to the road in question being classified as a highway, but in Scotland it would be classified as a road, whether that be either a public road or a private road. If the public right of passage is extinguished by a stopping up order, then something which was previously a road ceases to be so as the (literally) defining right of passage no longer exists (*Hamilton, supra*).

The question of the public right of passage figured prominently in the case of *Hamilton v Nairn* 2011 SC 49.

In that case, the respondents concluded missives to purchase a plot of land next to Culter House Road in Aberdeen in order to relocate their cattery and livery stables business and build a new house. They obtained planning permission for this development from Aberdeen City Council, together with the consent of the Council to improve the junction of the driveway of the property with the public road. This proposed improvement involved cutting across the verge of the road.

However, the Reclaimer purchased the verge across which the new access was to be formed, and sought to prevent the respondents from carrying out the work. The Respondents sought against the Reclaimer decrees of Declarator and Interdict in order to stop the Reclaimer from preventing the work. The Reclaimer's main argument was that the public right of way or passage extended only to the metalled surface of the road, on the basis that it was not used for passage by vehicles. That argument failed, first, because vehicles, did use the verge for passage, since the road was so narrow that vehicles required to use the verge to pass each other, and, in any event, because the requirement of section 151 is for a right of passage... *by whatever means,* which includes pedestrian use. The Reclaimer's subsidiary argument was that, if passage by pedestrians were relevant, nonetheless, the road, as defined by section 151, is limited to only those parts of the verge over which pedestrians walked.

At paragraph [26] the Court stated:

> "Such a proposition would appear to be contrary to the views expressed by Lord Skerrington in *McRobert v Reid* [1914 SC 633] (p 648):
>
>> 'There is not much authority in Scotland as to the extent and limits of the right enjoyed by the public in the different classes of highways, but, in my view, there is one quality which is essential and which must be common to all of them, viz., that the surface of a highway and every square inch of it belongs to the public, not, of course, in property, but in order that it may be used for certain purposes... The primary right of the public in a highway is that of passage, but if this point be kept in view, one may say, as Lord Curriehill did in *Waddell v Buchan* [(1868) 6 M 690 at 699], that 'the nature of the right is a right to use the surface for the purposes of locomotion.' In short, a member of the public has a *jus spatiandi* within

> the limits of a highway which he may exercise as he thinks fit, provided the eccentricity of his course does not disturb the public traffic or the public peace.'"

It is intended, in light of the above discussion, to consider the question of parking on highways and, in Scotland, roads.

Parking on Roads and Highways

As mentioned above, though a right of Highway (or right to use a road) is primarily a right of locomotion, other reasonable uses are permissible.

This was explored in the case of *D.P.P v Jones* [1999] 2 A.C. 240, a case which involved a peaceful protest on a highway adjacent to Stonehenge. Two of the organisers were arrested, charged and convicted of conducting a trespassory assembly on a highway, in respect of which there was in force an order under section 14A of the Public Order Act 1986. They appealed, ultimately, to the House of Lords.

The question, as articulated by Lord Irvine of Lairg LC (at page 258H) was:

> "whether the law today should recognise that the public highway is a public place, on which all manner of reasonable activities may go on."

The House decided by a majority of 3 to 2 that, in the particular circumstances of the case, no offence had been committed.

The divergence of views was interesting, and of some relevance to the question of whether vehicles might be parked on a highway, even although parking as such was not mentioned.

Lord Irvine of Lairg answered his own question at page 257D thus:

> "I conclude therefore the law to be that the public highway is a public place which the public may enjoy for any reasonable purpose, provided the activity in question does not amount to a public or private nuisance and does not obstruct the highway by unreasonably impeding the primary right of the public to pass and repass: within these qualifications there is a public right of peaceful assembly on the highway."

He added, at page 257H:

> Further, there can be no basis for distinguishing highways on publicly owned land and privately owned land. The nature of the public's right of use of the highway cannot depend upon whether the owner of the subsoil is a private landowner or a public authority. Any fear, however, that the rights of private landowners might be prejudiced by the right as defined are unfounded. The law of trespass will continue to protect private landowners against unreasonably large, unreasonably prolonged or unreasonably obstructive assemblies upon these highways."

Dissenting, Lord Slynn of Hadley, at page 264B, preferred to characterise the right as being "restricted to passage and reasonable incidental uses associated with passage."

Also dissenting, Lord Hope of Craighead referred to the dicta of Lord Esher MR in *Harrison v. Duke of Rutland* [1893] 1 Q.B. 142 at page 146:

> "Highways are, no doubt, dedicated *prima facie* for the purpose of passage; but things are done upon them by everybody which are recognised as being rightly done, and as constituting a reasonable and usual mode of using a highway *as such*. If a person on a highway does not transgress such reasonable and usual mode of using it, I do not think that he will be a trespasser."

Then, at page 274, he stated:

> "I think therefore that the law as stated by Lord Esher M.R. in *Harrison v. Duke of Rutland* [1893] 1 QB 142 can be taken to be the law as it must be applied between members of the public who seek to exercise the public's right of way on a highway and the occupier of the land which has been dedicated to that right. The question is one of degree. But the principle which must be applied is that the highway is for passage, and such other uses as may be made of it as of right must be capable of being recognised as a reasonable and usual mode of using the highway as such."

Lord Clyde, who was with the majority, did not go so far as Lord Irvine of Lairg in regarding the highway as, essentially, a public space, nor did he take the narrow view expressed by Lord Slynn that the uses should be restricted to uses which are "reasonably incidental" to passage. Rather, he preferred the formulation "subsidiary to the user for passage".

He stated, at page 279D:

> "The right to use a highway includes the doing of certain other things subsidiary to the user for passage. It is within the scope of the right that the traveller may stop for a while at some point along the way. If he wishes to refresh himself, or if there is some particular object which he wishes to view from that point, or if there is some particular association with the place which he wishes to keep alive, his presence on the road for that purpose is within the scope of the acceptable user of the road... So, as it seems to me, the particular purpose for which a highway may be used within the scope of the public's right of access includes a variety of activities, whether or not involving movement, which are consistent with what people reasonably and customarily do on a highway."

Finally, Lord Hutton, at page 285E endorsed the passage in *Halsbury's Laws of England, 4th ed. reissue, vol. 21*, pages. 77–78, para. 110 that the public right is a right to pass for legitimate travel. However, he was of the view that some extension of the public right was justifiable, in particular, "whether that right should be extended so that the public has a right in some circumstances to hold a peaceful assembly on the public highway provided that it does not obstruct the use of the highway." He expressed the view, at page 287C, that any enlarged uses should not be inconsistent with the maintenance of the paramount idea that the right of the public is that of passage. He also expressed the view that the law of trespass on the highway should be in conformity with the law relating to proceedings for wilful obstruction of the highway under section 137 of the Highways Act 1980.

Turning to the relevant statutory provisions, Part 9 of the Highways Act 1980, (sections 130 to 185) sets out a comprehensive set of provisions relating to lawful and unlawful interference with highways in England and Wales.

Section 137 (1) (referred to by Lord Hutton) provides:

> "137 *Penalty for wilful obstruction.*
>
> (1) If a person, without lawful authority or excuse, in any way wilfully obstructs the free passage along a highway he is guilty of an offence and liable to imprisonment for a term not exceeding 51 weeks or a fine or both."

Under section 137ZA, the court has power to order the removal of an obstruction if it is still in place following a conviction under section 137.

Section 149 provides:

> 149 *Removal of things so deposited on highways as to be a nuisance etc.*

> (1) If any thing is so deposited on a highway as to constitute a nuisance, the highway authority for the highway may by notice require the person who deposited it there to remove it forthwith and if he fails to comply with the notice the authority may make a complaint to a magistrates' court for a removal and disposal order under this section.
>
> (2) If the highway authority for any highway have reasonable grounds for considering—
>
>> (a) that any thing unlawfully deposited on the highway constitutes a danger (including a danger caused by obstructing the view) to users of the highway, and
>>
>> (b) that the thing in question ought to be removed without the delay involved in giving notice or obtaining a removal and disposal order from a magistrates' court under this section,
>
> the authority may remove the thing forthwith."

The subsequent subsections make provision for recovery of the costs of removal, authority for disposal etc.

The equivalent Scottish legislation is somewhat differently worded.

In particular, the *Roads (Scotland) Act 1984* by section 59 provides, in part:

> "59 *Control of obstructions in roads*
>
> (1) Subject to subsection (6) below, nothing shall be placed or deposited in a road so as to cause an obstruction except with the roads authority's consent in writing and in accordance with any reasonable conditions which they think fit to attach to the consent.

(2) A person who contravenes subsection (1) above commits an offence.

(3) Without prejudice to subsection (2) above, a person who contravenes subsection (1) above may be required by the roads authority or by a constable in uniform to remove the obstruction forthwith, and commits an offence if he fails to do so.

(4) Where —

>   (a) a requirement under subsection (3) above is not complied with;
>
>   (b) the person who placed or deposited the obstruction cannot be readily traced; or
>
>   (c) the case is one of emergency,

the roads authority or a constable may remove the obstruction (or cause it to be removed) and recover such expenses as are reasonably incurred in so doing from the said person."

Section 129 (2) provides:

> "(2) A person who, without lawful authority or reasonable excuse, places or deposits anything in a road so as to obstruct the passage of, or to endanger, road users commits an offence".

It will be noted that section 137 of the 1980 Act creates, in England, an offence of "wilful" obstruction, which, of course, requires *mens rea,* whereas, in Scotland, section 129 of the 1984 Act creates a strict liability offence. Section 149 of the 1980 Act approaches objects left in the road from the perspective of nuisance, whereas section 59 refers simply to causing an obstruction. Unlike section 149, breach of section 59 constitutes an offence, and gives wider powers of removal, not requiring judicial intervention and extending powers of removal to the police as well as the local authority.

Of more immediate applicability to parking is section 22 of the Road Traffic Act 1988 (which applies in both Scotland and England):

> "22 *Leaving vehicles in dangerous positions.*
>
> If a person in charge of a vehicle causes or permits the vehicle or a trailer drawn by it to remain at rest on a road in such a position or in such condition or in such circumstances as to involve a danger of injury to other persons using the road, he is guilty of an offence."

Section 99 of the Road Traffic Regulation Act 1984 (which applies in both England and Scotland) provides:

> "99 *Removal of vehicles illegally, obstructively or dangerously parked, or abandoned or broken down.*
>
> (1) The Secretary of State may by regulations make provision for the removal of vehicles which have been permitted to remain at rest—
>
> (a) on a road or other land in contravention of any statutory prohibition or restriction, or
>
> (b) on a road or other land in such a position or in such condition or in such circumstances as to cause obstruction to other persons using the road or land concerned or as to be likely to cause danger to such persons, or
>
> (c) on a road or on any land in the open air or other land

in such a position or in such condition or in such circumstances as to appear, to an authority empowered by the regulations to remove such vehicles, to have been abandoned without lawful authority,

(d) or which have broken down on a road or other land."

The relevant regulations are found in the *Removal and Disposal of Vehicles Regulations 1986/183* [as amended].

Also, Regulation 103 of the *Road Vehicles (Construction and Use) Regulations 1986/1078* provides:

"103. No person in charge of a motor vehicle or trailer shall cause or permit the vehicle to stand on a road so as to cause any unnecessary obstruction of the road."

Furthermore, the Highway Code at Rules 240 to 249 sets out a number of rules relating to stopping and parking, though these largely reflect the statutory and regulatory positions regarding parking. (See https://www.gov.uk/guidance/the-highway-code/waiting-and-parking-238-to-252#rule238).

Although local authorities may regulate parking under delegated powers (as discussed below) in Scotland, Part 6 of the Transport (Scotland) Act 2019 imposes a national ban on pavement parking, double parking and parking at dropped kerbs. The only power granted to local authorities being to designate certain exemptions – for example to ensure safe access for emergency vehicles.

In particular, section 50 provides:

"50 *Pavement parking prohibition*

(1) A person must not park a motor vehicle on a pavement (in this Part, this prohibition is referred to as the "pavement

parking prohibition").

(2) For the purposes of the pavement parking prohibition—

(a) a motor vehicle is parked on a pavement if—

(i) it is stationary, and

(ii) one or more of its wheels (or any part of them) is on any part of the pavement,

(b) a stationary motor vehicle is parked whether or not—

(i) the driver of the vehicle is in attendance at the vehicle,

(ii) the engine of the vehicle is running.

(3) The pavement parking prohibition is subject to the exceptions set out in section 55."

The definition of "motor vehicle" is wide enough to include motorcycles.

How, then does this body of authority relate to parking on a highway or other road?

Notwithstanding Lord Hutton's suggestion that the law on trespass on the highway should be in conformity with the law relating to proceedings for wilful obstruction of the highway under section 137 of the 1980 Act, there are plainly two (or, indeed, bearing in mind the difference between the English and Scottish regime), three different and complementary regimes in play.

At common law, the question is whether (to use Lord Irvine's test) parking is a reasonable purpose for which to use the road and, if so, whether a parked vehicle obstructs the highway by unreasonably impeding the primary right of the public to pass and repass; whether, if the analysis is properly that suggested by Lord Slynn, parking is "a reasonable incidental use associated with passage"; whether, as Lord Clyde suggests, parking is "subsidiary" to the right of passage; whether, as Lord Hope suggested, parking can be regarded as "a reasonable and usual mode of using the highway *as such;* or whether, as suggested by Lord Hutton, parking is "inconsistent with the maintenance of the paramount idea that the right of the public is that of passage".

It should also be borne in mind that the question cannot be "is parking in general permitted on a road or highway?" for the question must relate to whether a particular vehicle parked on a particular road can lawfully be there, and this, in part relates to whether or not it constitutes an obstruction to the free right of passage and may also be tied up with the question of the duration of the parking. This is an issue highlighted by Lord Clyde in *DPP v Jones* at page 280D:

> "Further, the public have no *jus manendi* on a highway, so that any stopping and standing must be reasonably limited in time. While the right may extend to a picnic on the verge, it would not extend to camping there."

This comment also serves to underline that the same rules apply to parking on the verge as they do to parking on the metalled roadway (see, also, *Hamilton v Nairn, supra*). Therefore, different instances of parking of different durations may or may not be lawful, depending on the facts and circumstances of the individual case. Furthermore, precisely the same instance of parking may or may not be lawful depending on which formulation of the test might be used.

However, these may be more theoretical rather than real problems, as the civil remedy would be either injunction or interdict, which may not normally be a realistic option. In the real world, an issue is more likely to arise if a car is parked on a highway or road so as to cause an obstruction to the free exercise of the right of passage, in which case the matter would fall to be dealt with under the appropriate statutory regime.

Private Roads over which there is no public right of passage

Where there is a private road over which there is no public right of passage, the position is a lot more straightforward. *Prima facie*, members of the public have no right to be on the road, and they have no right to park on the road. If they are parking on a private road, they will be trespassers and can be dealt with as such.

It might be, however, that they have legitimate business on the private road (for example, visiting premises adjacent to the road). In that event, they are present as licensees and what they can and cannot do will fall to be governed by the terms of their licence – verbal or written, express or implied.

However, even in what seems a straightforward case, there may be complications.

For example, in a case in the Sheriff Appeal Court, *Munro v Rose* (unreported, 7th April, 2022), the issue related to the circumstances in which a vehicle parked on a servitude right of access might constitute an obstruction.

The pursuer had obtained an interdict against the proprietor of adjacent land "by himself and by his servants and all others acting under his orders or on his behalf from trespassing or entering upon the [access road] so as to impede or obstruct the pursuer and his servants, customers and others in their use of [ground owned by the pursuer] for purposes including, but not limited to, parking, delivering and gaining access to [the pursuer's] shop premises adjacent to the said [ground] save insofar as [the defender] is entitled in terms of [a servitude right of access which he enjoyed over the pursuer's land]."

The pursuer brought proceedings against the defender for breach of interdict in circumstances in which the defender (who owned a garage) caused or permitted tankers to park on the access route in such a way that it was not possible for another vehicle to pass along the access route.

However, as recorded in paragraph [4] of the SAC's decision:

> "The sheriff found as proved various incidents between November 2018 and 6 July 2020 when vehicles visiting the respondent's garage were stationary on the access road, but that no person or vehicle was impeded or obstructed in any way by these vehicles. He concluded that there had been no breach of interdict arising from these incidents and therefore assoilzied the respondent."

In effect, what the Sheriff decided was that, even where it would not be possible for a vehicle to pass the tanker, there is no obstruction unless and until another vehicle turns up, tries, and fails to pass the tanker. The corollary would be that, as soon as the other vehicle gives up and goes away, the tanker would cease to be an obstruction until such time as a yet other vehicle turns up and fails to get past.

This seems a curious analysis, yet it was one with which the Sheriff Appeal Court found no fault, though it is notable that this was on the basis of a strict construction of the words of the interdict itself, so it is unclear how far another court, in different circumstances would take a similar view of what constitutes an obstruction.

Should a vehicle be parked on a private road (or, strictly, in Scotland a roadway which is not a "road" at all – see above) so as to cause an obstruction or should it appear to have been abandoned, it may be possible to have it removed under the *Removal and Disposal of Vehicles Regulations 1986*. As noted above the Regulations are made under section 99 of the Road Traffic Regulations Act 1984 which applies to both roads and "other land."

Local Authority Provision of Parking Facilities

The discussion so far has concerned parking on roads in respect of which there is no parking scheme in operation. However, local authorities are given powers under statute to provide both on-street and off-street parking.

Section 32 of *The Road Traffic Regulation Act 1984* (which applies in both Scotland and England) provides:

> "32 *Power of local authorities to provide parking places.*
>
> (1) Where for the purpose of relieving or preventing congestion of traffic it appears to a local authority to be necessary to provide within their area suitable parking places for vehicles, the local authority, subject to Parts I to III of Schedule 9 to this Act—
>
>> (a) may provide off-street parking places (whether above or below ground and whether or not consisting of or including buildings) together with means of entrance to and egress from them, or
>>
>> (b) may by order authorise the use as a parking place of any part of a road within their area, not being a road the whole or part of the width of which is within Greater London."

Section 35 (1) provides:

> (1) As respects any parking place—
>
>> (a) provided by a local authority under section 32 of this Act, or
>>
>> (b) provided under any letting or arrangements made by

a local authority under section 33(4) of this Act, the local authority, subject to Parts I to III of Schedule 9 to this Act, may by order make provision as to —

(i) the use of the parking place, and in particular the vehicles or class of vehicles which may be entitled to use it,

(ii) the conditions on which it may be used,

(iii) the charges to be paid in connection with its use (where it is an off-street one), and

(iv) the removal from it of a vehicle left there in contravention of the order and the safe custody of the vehicle and the power under paragraph (iii) to make provision as to the payment of charges shall include power to make provision requiring those charges, or any part of them, to be paid by means of the hire or purchase in advance, or the use, of parking devices in accordance with the order."

Further powers are conferred on local authorities in the remainder of section 35 for the providing of access to parking areas (section 35(2)), and the use of parking meters or similar devices such as cards, discs or the like (section 35(3), read along with section 35(3B)). It is noteworthy, however, that any device specified by a local authority must be one which has been prescribed by the Secretary of State by an Order made for the purposes of section 35.

Section 35A makes provision for offences and proceedings in respect of parking spaces, and, in this regard, it is worth singling out section 35A (5) which provides:

"(5) While a vehicle is within a parking place, it shall not be lawful for the driver or conductor of the vehicle, or for any

> person employed in connection with it, to ply for hire or accept passengers for hire; and if a person acts in contravention of this subsection he shall be guilty of an offence."

Given that Part IV of the Act is of an enabling nature (which would therefore permit local authorities to specify the activities forbidden in the car parking areas) the effect of subsection (5) is to embed the prohibition on plying for hire in the primary legislation, thereby depriving local authorities of any discretion to permit such activities in its car parks (though, of course, a local authority might separately designate taxi ranks).

Section 35B empowers the Secretary of State to make regulations as to the information required to be displayed by local authorities regarding car parking and section 35C empowers local authorities to vary charges for off-street parking by giving notice of the same, but with such notice being given in accordance with Regulations made by the Secretary of State.

Section 36 makes provision for on-street parking:

> "36. Provisions as to authorising use of roads for parking.
>
> (1) Subject to section 37 of this Act, no order under section 32(1)(b) of this Act shall—
>
> > (a) authorise the use of any part of a road so as unreasonably to prevent access to any premises adjoining the road or the use of the road by any person entitled to use it, or so as to be a nuisance, or
> >
> > (b) be made in respect of any part of a road without the consent of the authority or person responsible for the maintenance of the road.

(2) The exercise by a local authority of their powers under section 32 of this Act with respect to the use as a parking place of any part of a road shall not render them subject to any liability in respect of the loss of or damage to any vehicle or the fittings or contents of any vehicle parked in the parking place..."

Section 36 extends the powers of a local authority in relation to on-street parking to apply also to roads for which the Secretary of State is the Highways Authority, but only where "the order is, and is stated to be, made by virtue of this section and for the purposes of a general scheme of traffic control in a stated area".

Therefore, a local authority has wide powers to authorise the use of a road for on-street parking (section 32 (1)(b)). This power is not restricted to roads which the local authority has a duty to maintain (see section 36(1)(b)) – in the terminology of the section 151 of the 1984 Act "public roads" – but extends also to private roads, albeit with the consent of the person responsible for the maintenance of the road.

It is beyond the scope of the present work to look in detail at specific parking schemes which may have been promulgated by local authorities or individual Orders made by the Secretary of State under the above-mentioned powers, though of course, as with all delegated legislation, local parking and traffic schemes are susceptible, where appropriate, to judicial review – see, for example, *Freight Transport Association v Lothian Regional Council* 1977 SC 324.

CHAPTER TWO

PRIVATE CAR PARKS

The common starting point in both Scotland and England and Wales is that parking on another's land without permission constitutes a trespass. However, where the owner of land operates it as a car park, then that owner is, in law, granting a licence for persons to park on the land.

The licence might be granted to any member of the public, or restricted to members of the public driving particular types of vehicle (for example private cars but not commercial vehicles), or, indeed, restricted to particular classes of person – for example, guests at a hotel or pub or restaurant, shoppers at a supermarket, passengers at a railway station etc.

Thus, the relationship between the car park operator and the person parking the car is contractual and is governed by the terms of the contract in question. In any particular case, then, the answer to the question of which rules apply and how they might fall to be interpreted is generally found in contract law.

The first question to be considered is to determine which, if any conditions apply.

This is seen clearly in the case of *Thornton v Shoe Lane Parking* [1971] 2QB 163, where the plaintiff arrived at the entrance to a parking garage which was controlled by a traffic light. When, Mr. Thornton drove up to the red light, the machine at the entry issued a ticket, the light turned green, he drove into the garage, and the car was then parked by means of a stacking lift. When he came to collect the car, it rolled off the lift and injured his foot.

The defendant denied liability. On the bottom of the ticket, in small print, it stated that it was "issued subject to conditions ... displayed on the premises." On a pillar opposite the ticket machine there was a panel displaying eight printed "conditions", the second of which stated that the garage would not be liable for any injury to the customer occurring when the customer's car was on the premises.

The court treated the relationship between the customer and the garage as contractual, and decided the case in favour of Mr. Thornton on the basis of the well-established legal principles underlying other "ticket" cases. The Court of Appeal upheld that decision.

The starting point for Lord Denning M.R. (at page 169G) was that the offer had been accepted:

> "when Mr. Thornton drove up to the entrance and, by the movement of his car, turned the light from red to green, and the ticket was thrust at him. The contract was then concluded, and it could not be altered by any words printed on the ticket itself. In particular, it could not be altered so as to exempt the company from liability for personal injury due to their negligence."

In other words, it was simply too late for any additional terms to be incorporated into the contract. However, Lord Denning also analysed the case according to what he described as "the old fashioned ticket cases":

> "We then have to go back to the three questions put by Mellish LJ. in *Parker v. South Eastern Railway Co.*, 2 CP.D. 416, 423... the only condition that matters for this purpose is the exempting condition. It is no use telling the customer that the ticket is issued subject to some "conditions" or other, without more: for he may reasonably regard "conditions" in general as merely regulatory, and not as taking away his rights, unless the exempting condition is drawn specifically to his attention."

In this particular case, the exempting condition had not been drawn specifically to Mr. Thornton's attention and so did not apply to exempt the garage from liability.

The common law principles regarding the contract for parking have also been supplemented both by statute and "soft" rules such as industry Codes of Practice,

In particular, the British Parking Association, a trade association for parking companies, issues an Approved Operator Scheme Code of Practice, the latest version of which was issued in February, 2024. This has been superseded by the Association's new *Private Sector Single Code of Practice* which was published on 27th June 2024. Most of the provisions come into force on 1st October, 2024, with the Code due to be fully implemented by 31st December, 2026. The BPA Codes of Practice set out a detailed code of regulation governing signs, charges and enforcement procedures, and the Codes' provisions (though not having the force of law) form an integral component in the modern private parking regime, alongside the undernoted provisions of the Protections of Freedoms Act 2012 and the Transport (Scotland) Act 2019.

In England, Section 56 and Schedule 4 of the Protection of Freedoms Act 2012 makes provision for the recovery of unpaid parking charges from the registered keeper of a vehicle.

Paragraph 1(1) of Schedule 4 provides:

> "1(1) This Schedule applies where—
>
> (a) the driver of a vehicle is required by virtue of a relevant obligation to pay parking charges in respect of the parking of the vehicle on relevant land; and
>
> (b) those charges have not been paid in full.
>
> (2) It is immaterial for the purposes of this Schedule whether or not the vehicle was permitted to be parked (or to remain

parked) on the land."

Paragraph 4 gives a right under certain conditions to the creditor in a Parking Charge to recover any unpaid parking charges from the keeper of the vehicle. The Schedule then goes on to lay down certain conditions as to the exercise of that right, the giving of notices etc.

Similar provisions are made for Scotland by Part 8 [sections 90 to 108] of the Transport (Scotland) Act 2019.

In order for the statutory scheme to be effective, the DVLA has to disclose the contact details of the registered keeper to the parking operator who is the creditor under the parking charge. This is permitted under regulation 27 of the *Road Vehicles (Registration and Licensing) Regulations 2002 (SI 2002/2742)*, which empowers the Secretary of State to make available particulars in the vehicle register to anyone who has reasonable cause for wanting the particulars to be made available to him. In the case of parking enforcement, the policy of the Secretary of State is to do so only to members of an accredited trade association. The criteria for accreditation were stated in Parliament to include the existence of a clear and enforced code of conduct (for example relating to conduct, parking charge signage, charge levels, appeals procedure, approval of ticket wording and appropriate pursuit of penalties (See *Hansard (HC Debates)*, 24 July 2006, col 95WS)

The practical effect is that it is only members of an accredited trade association who can use the statutory provisions to recover unpaid parking fees. The outcome is that, for private car parks, the effect of the Code and statutory provisions read together is to produce a statutory regime analogous to local authority schemes.

One particular perceived abuse was the clamping by private operators of vehicles as a means of enforcement of private parking schemes.

The analysis at common law which had been adopted by English Courts was that, where a notice warns of certain consequences, such as wheel clamping in the event of unauthorised parking, then, if the driver has seen the sign, yet parks, that operates as implied consent to the clamping of the vehicle. Thus, in *Arthur v Anker* [1997] QB 564, Sir Thomas Bingham MR stated (at page 573B):

> "It is enough at this point to say that by voluntarily accepting the risk that his car might be clamped Mr. Arthur also, in my view, accepted the risk that the car would remain clamped until he paid the reasonable cost of clamping and declamping. He consented not only to the otherwise tortious act of clamping the car but also to the otherwise tortious action of detaining the car until payment."

However, there were limits on this principle. In particular, the judge went on to say that he would not accept that the clamper could exact any unreasonable or exorbitant charge for releasing the car, and the court would be very slow to find implied acceptance of such an excessive charge. He also stated that the clamper could not justify any delay in releasing the car after the owner offered to pay, and a means had to be provided for the owner to communicate his offer to pay.

In Scotland, by contrast, according to the High Court in *Black and Penrice v Carmichael* 1992 SLT 897, implied consent to and acceptance of the risk of clamping was, and is a legal theory which does not apply, irrespective of what any notice may say.

In the *Black* case, two notices were displayed in a private car park, which stated:

> "Private Property—unauthorised and unlawfully parked vehicles will be immobilised and a levy of £45 charged for release. South Coast Security (0506-873077). Agents to the Owner."

Two cars were parked in the car park without authority. They were each clamped and a notice affixed to their windscreens stating:

> "Notice of Levy on trespass Parking. This vehicle has been parked on private property without the permission of the owner of that property, despite a prominently displayed warning sign. Having parked there and having seen the notice you have consented to the risk of immobilisation and the levy of £45 for release."

The clampers were charged with extortion and, in the alternative, theft. The Sheriff found the charge of extortion relevant and the charge of theft irrelevant. Both the accused and the Procurator Fiscal cross-appealed to the High Court, which found both charges to be relevant.

Lord Justice General Hope at page 900D stated:

> "In my opinion, it is extortion to seek to enforce a legitimate debt by means which the law regards as illegitimate, just as it is extortion to seek by such means to obtain money or some other advantage to which the accused has no right at all. Furthermore, the only means which the law regards as legitimate to force a debtor to make payment of his debt are those provided by due legal process."

He continued at page 900I:

> I have every sympathy with landowners who find it intolerable that others should park their motor vehicles without permission on their private property. But I am not persuaded that the means which have been selected in this case to deter that activity can be regarded as legitimate. On the contrary it seems to me that they fall plainly within the proper limits of the crime of extortion, since the whole purpose of the wheel clamping as described in each charge was to obtain money as a condition of the release of the vehicle..."

and at page 900L, he added:

> The essential step in the argument, which makes the practice of wheel clamping illegal on the ground of extortion unless authorised by statute, is that it amounts to a demand for payment accompanied by the threat that until payment the vehicle will not be released."

It might be thought that a case where, as here, the driver was present on the land without the owner's consent might be distinguished from a case where (as in *Arthur,* above) the car was on the land on a contractual basis, though the driver then overstayed or failed to pay. However, this was a distinction which Lord Hope was not prepared to make. He stated, at page 900K, that it would not matter if the landowner had been entitled to be paid a parking charge:

> "...it would be quite irrelevant as a defence to the charge of extortion to show that the sum sought to be recovered by the wheel clamping was a legitimate charge for parking the car, and I agree with him that the accused must be taken to have been involved at least art and part in the charge of extortion since they are said to have affixed the clamp and put the notice on the windscreen."

The charge of theft was also relevant as clamping deprived the owner of the use of his vehicle.

Black was considered by the Lord Bingham MR in *Arthur v Anker* (supra) at pages 576H to page 578, but the judge referred to the definition of Blackmail in section 21 of the Theft Act 1968, and determined that, since the defendant (in the words of section 21) held the belief that he had reasonable grounds for making the demand; and that the use of the menaces was a proper means of reinforcing the demand, he would not be guilty of blackmail. Accordingly, there was an implied acceptance of the risk of clamping.

Insofar as these decisions could be reconciled, it seemed to be that implied consent cannot be given to being made the victim of a crime, but, in Scotland, clamping is a crime, whereas in England it was not.

In *Vine v Waltham Forest Borough Council* [2000] 1WLR 2383, (which related to an incident which had occurred in 1997) a driver had been taken ill and pulled into a private car parking space in order to vomit by the roadside. She parked within sight of a sign which read:

> "Any vehicle left unattended is liable to be towed away or wheel clamped. Recoverable by payment of a fine of £105."

She returned to find the car clamped and she had to pay the fine to secure its release, She sued for damages for wrongful detention of the car.

The Court of Appeal affirmed the principle that the act of clamping the wheel of a car, even when it was trespassing, was a tortious act of trespass to its owner's property unless it could be shown that the owner had consented to or willingly assumed the risk of his car being clamped. However, the corollary of that was that, if the person doing the clamping could not establish that the car owner saw and understood the significance of the warning notice, he could be liable to the owner in damages. In the particular case, the Recorder had made an explicit finding that the plaintiff had not seen the sign, and, therefore ought not to have "jumped to the conclusion that the plaintiff had consented to, or willingly assumed, the risk of her car being clamped". (Per Roche LJ at page 2390 D-G)

The outcome of these cases was that wheel clamping by private actors as a means of parking enforcement was always a crime in Scotland, whereas, in England, it was at least capable of being regarded as a legitimate means of parking control, although *Vine* perhaps represented the early stages of a process to rein in possible abuses. It was not, however, a satisfactory state of affairs.

However, this was a process which did not get a chance to continue because of a conscious decision on the part of Parliament, as a result of the reform of private parking regimes referred to above, at a stroke rendered wheel clamping by private actors in England unlawful. In particular, by section 52 of the Protection of Freedoms Act 2012 (which applies only in England and Wales) provides:

> "(1) A person commits an offence who, without lawful authority—
>
>> (a) immobilises a motor vehicle by the attachment to the vehicle, or a part of it, of an immobilising device, or
>>
>> (b) moves, or restricts the movement of, such a vehicle by any means,
>
> intending to prevent or inhibit the removal of the vehicle by a person otherwise entitled to remove it."

In order to meet the contractual defence of implied consent, section 51(2) provided that express or implied consent would not constitute lawful authority for the purposes of subsection (1); but subsection (3) permits restriction of movement by a fixed barrier where the barrier was in place (whether or not lowered) when the vehicle was parked.

This reformed parking regime came under scrutiny in the case of *Parking Eye Ltd. v Beavis; Cavendish Square Holding BV v Makdessi Parking Eye Ltd v Beavis (Consumers Association intervening)* [2016] AC 272 (hereafter referred to as *Beavis*).

In the *Beavis* case, each of the Defendants had parked in a shopping centre car park operated on behalf of the land's owners by the Claimant company. There was no charge for parking, but there was a maximum parking time of two hours, after which a parking charge was levied by the Claimant company. The Claimant received no payment from the owner of the car park, but, rather itself paid the owner for the right to operate the car park. It derived its income solely from the Charges which it levied.

The parking restriction was set out on a number of signs distributed around the car park and the Defendants did not dispute that the signs were reasonably large, prominent and legible, so that any reasonable user of the car park, including themselves, would be aware of their existence and nature and would have a fair opportunity to read them if they wished.

Each of the defendants had parked for a period in excess of two hours, as detected by automatic number plate recognition cameras in the car park. The Claimant was not in a position to tell who had actually parked the vehicle, but received from the DVLA the details of the Registered Keepers. It then exercised its Schedule 4 rights by sending to the Registered Keepers notices stating:

- that a Parking Charge of £85 was payable within 28 days of the date of the Notice, but would be discounted to £50 if paid within 14 days;

- that the charge was payable by the driver, but that under Para.9 (2) of Schedule 4 to the protection of Freedoms Act 2012 it would after 29 days be payable by the registered keeper if the driver had not by then paid or at least been identified to Parking Eye by the keeper,

- instructions for payment by internet, telephone or post.

Charges of £85 each were duly levied on the registered keepers, but remained unpaid. The Claimant duly brought small claims in the County Court, by way of test cases.

At first instance (see *Parking Eye Ltd v Beavis*, 2014 WL 8103800 (2014) at paragraph [17]) the Defendant raised a number of objections, including the following:

(i) No contract for parking was entered into;

(ii) Parking Eye has no standing to bring a claim;

(iii) The charge purports to be for breach but is not a genuine pre-estimate of loss;

(iv) The driver cannot be deemed to have agreed to the terms;

(v) The Claimant has not complied with the 2012 Act;

(vi) The charge is an unenforceable penalty.

The judge took *Thornton v Shoe Lane Parking* as his starting point, holding that, even although no ticket was issued, there was a valid contract constituted by unequivocal acceptance made manifest by driving in and parking his car. (paragraph [19]).

The Claimant argued that there was no consideration as there was no charge for the first two hours of parking (an argument which would not have been available had the events taken place in Scotland, where, of course, consideration is not required for there to be a binding contract). In any event, that argument failed on the basis that the driver's binding promise to leave after two hours, which failing to pay the charge was itself sufficient consideration. (paragraph [20])

The next argument was that the Claimant Company did not give any consideration as it was not itself the owner of the land and so, it was said, was in no position to grant a licence to occupy the land. The judge, however, pointed out that the owner was in a position to assign or licence to a third party (such as the Claimant) to grant a right to park on the land (and, in terms of the contract between the owner and the Claimant, this was what the owner had done). (Paragraphs [21] and [22])

The judge continued (at [27]):

> For those reasons I conclude that in these two cases Parking Eye was entitled to and did contract with the motorists as principal, not as agent for the landowner, and is lawfully entitled to sue them for the charges in its own name and keep

the proceeds for itself..."

The defendant then tried to argue that the Claimant was not the "creditor" under Schedule 4 of the 2012 Act, but this argument failed because the court had already reached the conclusion at [27] that the Claimant did have a right to payment.

The defendant also argued that the obligation to pay a parking charge was, by virtue of Regulation 8 of the Unfair Terms in Consumer Contracts Regulations 1999/2083 not binding on the defendants by reason that the term had the object or effect of "requiring any consumer who fails to fulfil his obligation to pay a disproportionately high sum in compensation".

This argument piggy-backed on the question whether, at common law, the parking charge was in reality a penalty, rather than a genuine pre-estimate of loss. The judge stated, at paragraph [47]:

> "It appears to me on the basis of the above authorities that the proper modern approach to deciding whether any particular clause is unenforceable as a penalty must be a global one, examining the clause from three overlapping perspectives: i. proportionality to actual loss; ii. tendency to deter rather than compensate; and iii. commercial justification/fairness, with a view to deciding whether, considered in the round, it is so extravagant, unconscionable and unjustifiable that the courts ought not to give effect to it."

and at paragraph [51]:

> "... my overall conclusion is that, although there is a sense in which this contractual parking charge has the characteristics of a deterrent penalty. It is neither improper in its purpose nor manifestly excessive in its amount. It is commercially justifiable, not only from the viewpoints of the landowner

and Parking Eye, but also from that of the great majority of motorists who enjoy the benefit of free parking at the site, effectively paid for by the minority of defaulters, who have been given clear notice of the consequences of over-staying."

The eventual appeal to the UK Supreme Court focussed on the penalty clause argument (and, indeed, was heard alongside another appeal which raised a similar issue).

Despite arguments presented to it radically to reform (or even abolish) the penalty rule, the UKSC took a more subtle approach.

This is seen most clearly in the Judgment of Lord Mance who suggested that the apparent dichotomy between a pre-estimate of loss and a penalty may be a false dichotomy. He suggested, at paragraph [152] that "There may be interests beyond the compensatory which justify the imposition on a party in breach of an additional financial burden." He went on to say:

> "What is necessary in each case is to consider, first, whether any (and if so what) legitimate business interest is served and protected by the clause, and, second, whether, assuming such an interest to exist, the provision made for the interest is nevertheless in the circumstances extravagant, exorbitant or unconscionable."

In light of these general observations, he went on, in the context of the *Beavis* appeal, first, to affirm the judge's contractual analysis, and then, in light of that, to say that the penalty doctrine was potentially applicable to the parking scheme (paragraph [193]) but that (at paragraph [197]):

> "In judging whether Parking Eyes parking charges fall foul of the penalty doctrine, the scheme it operates has to be seen as a whole, bearing in mind all the interests obviously involved."

At paragraph [199], he concluded that:

> "What matters is that a charge of the order of £85 (reducible on prompt payment) is an understandable ingredient of a scheme serving legitimate interests. Customers using the car park agree to the scheme by doing so. The position was well summed up by Judge Moloney QC, at para 7.16, when he said that:
>
>> 'although there is a sense in which this contractual parking charge has the characteristics of a deterrent penalty, it is neither improper in its purpose nor manifestly excessive in its amount. It is commercially justifiable, not only from the viewpoints of the landowner and Parking Eye, but also from that of the great majority of motorists who enjoy the benefit of free parking at the site, effectively paid for by the minority of defaulters, who have been given clear notice of the consequences of overstaying!'".

A similar approach was taken by the other judges, including Lord Neuberger of Abbotsbury PSC and Lord Sumption JSC in a joint judgment (with whom Lord Carnwath JSC concurred).

The core of their reasoning is found at paragraphs [98] to [100]. In particular, at paragraph [99], they said:

> "In our opinion, while the penalty rule is plainly engaged, the £85 charge is not a penalty. The reason is that although ParkingEye was not liable to suffer loss as a result of overstaying motorists, it had a legitimate interest in charging them which extended beyond the recovery of any loss. The scheme in operation here (and in many similar car parks) is that the landowner authorises ParkingEye to control access to the car park and to impose the agreed charges, with a view to managing the car park in the interests of the retail outlets,

their customers and the public at large. That is an interest of the landowners because (i) they receive a fee from ParkingEye for the right to operate the scheme, and (ii) they lease sites on the retail park to various retailers, for whom the availability of customer parking was a valuable facility. It is an interest of ParkingEye, because it sells its services as the managers of such schemes and meets the costs of doing so from charges for breach of the terms (and if the scheme was run directly by the landowners, the analysis would be no different). As we have pointed out, deterrence is not penal if there is a legitimate interest in influencing the conduct of the contracting party which is not satisfied by the mere right to recover damages for breach of contract."

The judges were also unanimous in finding that the parking charges did not fall foul of the Unfair Terms in Consumer Contracts Regulations 1999.

The outcome is that, although each case will require to be judged on its own facts and circumstances, it is likely that most schemes operated by members of the BPA are unlikely to be problematic.

One factor which was remarked upon by Lords Neuberger of Abbotsbury and Lord Sumption in the *Beavis* case was the statutory/regulatory context and the measure of indirect regulation though the BPA Code of Practice, the analogous provisions of regulated local authority schemes (see paragraphs [95] and [96]) and the outlawing of clamping.

One gets a strong sense that the courts' accommodation with private parking schemes (or at least those to which the BPA Code of Practice applies) derives from increasing confidence that the industry is increasingly properly regulated.

Most recently, Parliament has taken steps to put the regulation of private parking operators on a statutory basis. The Parking (Code of Practice) Act 2019 (which extends to both England and Wales and Scotland) makes provision for the Secretary of State to prepare a code of practice containing guidance about the operation and management of private parking facilities. Section 5 provides as follows:

> "5 *Effect of parking code*
>
> (1) A failure on the part of any person to act in accordance with any provision of the parking code does not of itself make that person liable to any legal proceedings in any court or tribunal.
>
> (2) But the Secretary of State must have regard to a failure to act in accordance with the parking code when deciding—
>
> > (a) whether to disclose any particulars contained in the register to a person under regulation 27 of the Road Vehicles (Registration and Licensing) Regulations 2002 (S.I. 2002/2742);
> >
> > (b) whether a person should be, or should continue to be, an accredited parking association."

Section 7 enables the Secretary of State to make provision for the appointment of an independent person to deal with appeals against parking charges, and section 8 permits the Secretary of State to make Regulations to impose levies on accredited parking associations to cover administrative and investigation costs.

The Parking (Code of Practice) Act 2019 (Commencement) Regulations 2024 (SI 2024 No 653) brought the Act into force on 20th May, 2022. The Regulations remain to be promulgated although the Government had previously published a draft statutory Code of Practice which had subsequently been withdrawn. Accordingly, one must look to the BPA's codes of Practice. The downside of this, however, is that the provisions of the Codes do not apply to operators who are not members of the association, though it may well be the aspiration of the BPA that its Code will come to enjoy a similar persuasive status to that of the Highway Code.

CHAPTER THREE

PRIVATE PARKING RIGHTS: THE SERVITUDE OF PARKING

Introduction

Sitting alongside the rights of members of the public to park on the road, in public car parks and on private land such as dedicated car parks, whether by common law right, under a statutory or regulatory scheme, or by way of contractual licence, there is a parallel universe of private rights to park on land belonging to others, whether by way or servitude or lease or rights deriving from common or shared ownership.

The law in this area, especially in relation to servitudes has, historically, not been clear, and even the watershed case of *Moncrieff v Jamieson* 2008 SC (HL) 1; 2007 1 WLR 2620 did not by any means resolve all the outstanding issues: although the consensus has moved to broad acceptance of the existence in the law of both Scotland and England of a servitude or easement of parking, to be strictly accurate, what Moncrieff decided was that the right to park a vehicle could exist as an *accessory* right to another servitude, such as a servitude of access. That said, there were strong and persuasive obiter dicta from several of the judges; but this has led to a few sporadic and so far unsuccessful attempts to push back against the concept of parking as servitude in its own right.

More contentious are questions of where parking ends and where storage begins, and whether the distinction matters – a question tied up with the related question of whether there is, in any event, a servitude of storage. These are themselves which engage what English law describes as the "ouster principle".

These questions in the common law sit alongside a relatively new system of statutory servitudes in Scotland and proposals from the Law Commission of England and Wales to abolish the ouster principle.

Beside Servitudes, the leasing of parking spaces presents an altogether simpler landscape, but some of the problems arising in relation to Servitudes spill over into parking rights created by lease or licence.

Finally, there may be issues arising from parking on unadopted roads where individual proprietors have joint or common ownership or a common interest in the *solum* of the road.

Thus, the first matter to be considered is parking as a Servitude or Easement.

Servitudes in General

The law of Scotland relating to servitudes has its roots in Roman Law. However, the servitude of parking does not appear to have been a servitude known in the civil law, though, curiously there is a passage in the *Digest* which mandates that the standard width of a road should be increased from 12 feet to 16 feet on a band to facilitate the turning of carts:

> "*Viae latitudo ex lege duodecim tabularum in porrectum octo pedes habet, in anfractum, id est ubi flexum est, sedecim.*"
> (Dig.8.3.8 Gaius 7 ad ed. provinc.)

That said, the absence of mention of parking could simply be, as Lord Roger of Earlsferry pointed out in *Moncrieff v Jamieson* at paragraph [73]:

> The problem does not feature in the Digest — but that may just be due to an accident of the compilers' work in reducing the jurists' writings for inclusion in the Digest. Your Lordships were not referred to any later civil law discussion.

Certainly, the mere fact that a right equivalent to parking was not recognised as a praedial servitude by Roman law would not, of itself, prevent Scots law from recognising such a servitude, just as it has recognised, for instance, a praedial servitude to take coal and a praedial servitude of fuel, feal and divot, neither of which was recognised by Roman law."

In any event, Scots law the Scots law of servitudes historically has developed through case law incrementally and in response to changing conditions.

For example, *Dyce v Hay* (1852) 1 Macq 305, was a case which originated in Scotland, in which the pursuers claimed that the public at large had a right to use a strip of land for recreation. This case, therefore, concerned a claimed public right, rather than a private servitude right. However, Lord Chancellor St. Leonards stated (at page 312):

> "there is no rule in the law of Scotland which prevents modern inventions and new operations being governed by old and settled legal principles. Thus, when the art of bleaching came into use, there was nothing in its novelty which should exclude it from the benefit of a servitude or easement, if such servitude or easement on other legal grounds was maintainable. The category of servitudes and easements must alter and expand with the changes that take place in the circumstances of mankind. The law of this country, as well as the law of Scotland, frequently moulds its practical operation without doing any violence to its original principles."

In the case of *Harvey v Lindsay* (1853) 15D 768 Lord Ivory stated at page 775:

> "I go quite along with the observations which have been made in recent cases, that we are not to limit servitudes to those already known and recognised in law, as in the progress

of society alterations may take place, and new servitudes may arise. The best recognised servitudes must at some time have been new."

Similarly, the Law of England relating to easements has roots in Roman Law, as pointed out by Evershed MR in *In re Ellenborough Park* [1956] Ch 131 at pages 162-163, and has enjoyed a similar incremental development through case law in response to changing conditions. It is significant that in *Dyce v Hay*, Lord St. Leonards explicitly equiparated the law of Scotland with the law of England in that respect, and this passage was quoted with approval by the Privy Council in *Attorney General of Southern Nigeria v. John Holt & Co. (Liverpool) Ltd.* [1915] AC 599 (P.C.) at page 617.

This is not to say that Scots Law relating to servitudes and English Law relating easements are identical. For example, in relation to prescriptive possession, Scots law is predicated on the concept of implied grant, whereas English law proceeds on the basis of presumed grant (*Carstairs v. Spence* 1924 SC 380 (2nd Division) per Lord Blackburn at pages 394 – 395). However, provided that one remains alert to such differences, there is, in the law of servitudes, a commonality at the level of principle amongst Scots, English and Commonwealth caselaw decisions which enables the subject to be treated in the round, albeit being alert as to where there may be scope for differences.

Having said all that, and despite the common sentiment mentioned above that the book of servitudes is not closed, last new servitude to have been declared in Scotland (at any rate prior to *Moncrieff*) was the Servitude of Bleaching (*Sinclair v Magistrates of Dysart* (1779) Mor 14519.) The Scottish Law Commission noted in its *Report on Real Burdens* (*Scot Law Com No. 181 – published October, 2000*) at paragraph 12.22:

"There is, in effect, a fixed list of servitudes in Scotland, derived mainly from Roman law, and despite *obiter dicta* to the contrary the courts have not generally been willing to add to the list. No new servitude has been recognised for 200 years, and the law of servitudes seems to have stopped when the law of real burdens began, in the closing years of the eighteenth century."

The law prior to Moncrieff v Jamieson

Prior to *Moncrieff* it had been a matter of some contention whether a servitude of parking was known to the law of Scotland. Academic commentary on this was largely sceptical (see, for example, the discussion in Cusine & Paisley *Servitudes and Rights of Way* (1998) at §3.45 to §3.52) and the case law at best equivocal.

In *Murrayfield Ice Rink Ltd. v Scottish Rugby Union Trustees* 1973 SC 21 the Feu Charter in favour of the Applicants (Murrayfield Ice Rink) contained a specific grant of what was described as a servitude of parking (set out on page 23 of the case report):

> "It is hereby declared that the servitude right of use for a Car Park affecting the Car Park Area hereinbefore mentioned is granted to the feuars as a pertinent of the feu and shall be inalienable by them as a separate tenement and shall be held by them only so long as they remain proprietors of the feu."

At the foot of page 31, Lord Justice-Clerk Grant commented that this was not a right of ownership, but a "mere servitude right". There was, however, no discussion as to whether it was actually capable of constituting a servitude.

The case of *Davidson v Wiseman* 2001 GWD 9-317, Banff Sheriff Court (13th February, 2001), concerned a failed attempt to establish a right of pedestrian and vehicular access. There had also been an ineptly pleaded attempt to set up a servitude right to park. Commenting on this, Sheriff Cusine did not comment upon whether there could be a servitude where a servitude right of vehicular access could not be established, a servitude right to parking could not be established either. It is inherent in this analysis that a servitude of parking as such could not exist – it could exist only as an accessory to a servitude right of access.

The possible acceptance of parking as an accessory right was recognised by Lady Smith in *Nationwide Building Society v Walter D Allan Ltd.* (Court of Session, 4th August, 2004) though she also appeared to close the door firmly on parking as a servitude in its own right. She stated at paragraph [26]:

> "I cannot conclude that Scots Law recognises, in principle, a servitude right of parking independent of any right of access."

The position in England was that parking as an easement in its own right was at least closer to general acceptance. In *Bilkus v London Borough of Redbridge* (1968) 207 EG 803 there was a covenant for parking, which was stated by Buckley J to have as its effect the conferring of an easement of parking (page 804, column 2). In *Patel and others v W. H. Smith (Eziot) Ltd and another* [1987] 1 WLR 853 it was common ground between the parties that an easement to park cars in a defined area is a right known to the law (at page 859H). In *London & Blenheim Estates Ltd. v Ladbroke Retail Parks Ltd.* [1992] 1 WLR 1278, in an *obiter* passage at pages 1285 to 1288, there is a careful review of authority by Judge Paul Barker QC who, under reference to *Bilkus v London Borough of Redbridge*, stated at page 1287H:

> "That is a clear authority that in some circumstances the right to park cars can amount to an easement."

On appeal, (*London & Blenheim Estates Ltd. v Ladbroke Retail Parks Ltd.* [1994] 1 WLR 31 at page 38), the Court of Appeal declared it unnecessary to reach a view on the question.

In *Redland Aggregates Limited v Dace* (unreported) Court of Appeal (Civil Division), 11th October, 1996, although a claim for an easement of parking failed, no point was taken that such an easement was unknown to the law.

At first instance in *Batchelor v Marlow and another* (unreported) Chancery Division (11th May, 2000) the judge, Mr. Nicholas Warren QC, relying on *London & Blenheim Estates* found established a prescriptive easement of parking; at Appeal (*Batchelor v Marlow and another* [2003] 1 WLR 764) it was common ground that the right to park could exist as an easement, at any rate if expressly granted – see page 766 at paragraph 4. However, in the leading judgment, Tucky LJ stated, at paragraphs 18 and 19:

> "18. If one asks the simple question: 'Would the plaintiff - have any reasonable use of the land for parking?' the answer, I think, must be 'No'. He has no use at all during the whole of the time that parking space is likely to be needed. But if one asks the question whether the plaintiff has any reasonable use of the land for any other purpose, the answer is even clearer. His right to use his land is curtailed altogether for intermittent periods throughout the week. Such a restriction would, I think, make his ownership of the land illusory.
>
> 19. I therefore accept Miss Williamson's submissions on this aspect of the case. It follows that I do not think the right found to exist by the deputy judge was capable of being an easement..."

In *K-Sultana Saeed v Plustrade Ltd.* [2001] EWCA Civ 2011 a tenant was granted a right under her lease along with other tenants "to park on such part of the retained property as may from time to time be specified by the lessor as reserved for car parking, subject to such regulations as the lessor may make from time to time." She and the other tenants parked on an area which had been designated for parking and which had 13 spaces available. The Lessor then blocked off that area to prevent anyone from parking there. Instead, he offered the tenants an alternative area which had only 4 spaces available.

The entitlement or otherwise of the Lessor to do this is discussed below, but the significance of this case to the present discussion is that the Claimant, a tenant, argued that the right which she had was an easement. However, the core question in the case was whether the Lessor had substantially interfered with the tenant's right to park, but, in order to answer that question, it was not necessary to determine the precise nature of the right. Sir Christopher Slade stated, at paragraph [22]:

> "There has in the past been some doubt as to whether a right to park in a car park can exist in law as an easement. More recent authorities of courts of first instance, cited by Judge Paul Baker, Q.C. in *London and Blenheim Estates Ltd v. Ladbroke Retail Parks Ltd* [1994] 1 W.L.R. 31 at page 36, and his own decision in that case appear to establish that it can, provided only that it does not amount to a claim to the entire beneficial user of the servient area, in which case the grant would not be that of an easement, though it might be of some larger or different grant; see also *Batchelor v. Murphy [sic]* May 11, 2000, unreported. However, the Court of Appeal in the first mentioned case identified, but did not answer, the question whether the right to park could exist as a valid easement and no other Court of Appeal decision relating to the question has been cited to us. In the circumstances and in the absence of full argument, I would prefer to leave the question open, without intending in any way to suggest that Judge Paul Baker, Q.C.'s decision was wrong."

The position, then, on the eve of *Moncrieff* was that, in Scotland, there was some judicial support for a parking as an accessory right to a servitude right of vehicular access but strong resistance to it as a servitude in its own right. In England, the courts seemed to be on the cusp of declaring the existence of an easement of parking, but no court had been quite prepared to go all the way. At the same time, there was lurking in the background the question, mentioned in other cases, but articulated strongly by the

Court of Appeal in *Batchelor v Marlow* of whether a right of parking (whether standalone or accessory) was so great as to deprive the owner of the servient tenement of any reasonable use of his land, so as to make his ownership illusory – the so-called ouster principle.

These are the themes which played out in *Moncrieff v Jamieson*.

Moncrieff v Jamieson

The facts

The pursuers, Mr. and Mrs. Moncrieff, lived on an island in the Shetland archipelago. Their house, "Da Store" was a former shop (which had closed in 1927) and which was situated at the foot of a cliff. Historically, access was had to it from the sea by boat. On the landward side, the only way to get down to Da Store was by means of a narrow staircase, which led from the land belonging to the defenders at the top of the cliff. That land, which sloped downwards to the cliff edge, was a large open area which had situated on it, some distance uphill, the house which had been occupied by the defender and his family. Yet further uphill ran the public road. The clifftop had been reached by a road which had fallen into disrepair, to the extent that goods reached the clifftop from the public road by means of a system of ropes and pulleys.

The land at the top of the cliff and Da Store had originally been in common ownership, but, in 1973, the title was split, a Disposition of Da Store being granted by the common owner in favour of the pursuers' predecessor in title. Because Da Store had no direct access to the system of public roads that served the community in that part of Shetland, among the rights conveyed by the Disposition, to be enjoyed together with the lands on which Da Store was situated, was the following: "(Fourth) a right of access from the branch public road through Sandsound."

No route was specified. Over the years, a private road had been formed, and its route adjusted from time to time by agreement between the pursuers as proprietors of the dominant tenement and the defender as proprietor of the servient tenement. By the time the dispute arose the clifftop was reached by a boomerang-shaped road which ran steeply downhill for some 150 yards from the public road. There was a garden in front of the defenders' house, which was fenced off by a drystane dyke. The pursuers and other visitors to the dominant tenement drove down to the cliff edge and parked on the servient tenement in an area in the vicinity of the top of the stairs. They were able to do so as the stone wall had a kink at its foot so as to create an open area where the parking could take place. Persons then going down to Da Store did so on foot by descending the stairs.

All was well for a number of years until Mrs. Jameson decided that she wanted a square garden, which necessitated rebuilding the wall by removing the kink. One morning, the pursuer found himself unable to park because the area was blocked by a pile of stones, and would become permanently inaccessible as a result of the rebuilding of the wall. The scene was set: or, as Sheriff C. Scott Mackenzie at first instance (2004 SCLR 135 at page 185) quoted:

> "*Facilis descensus Averno: Noctes atque dies patet atri ianua Ditis; Sed revocare gradum...hoc opus, hic labor est*" (Virgil, *Aeneid, vi, 126*)

The Issues

The core issue was whether the Sheriff was correct in finding that, in this case, the right to park existed as an accessory right to the servitude right of vehicular access. The majority in the Inner House of the Court of Session found that he was.

Inherent in this issue was the question of whether a right to park was capable of being a right accessory to a servitude of access – the point being that vehicular access to a dominant tenement normally entails vehicles gaining access to the dominant tenement, so there would not normally be any need for vehicles to park on the servient tenement.

However, the Sheriff had also found that a servitude right of parking had been established alternatively and independently of the specific grant in the Disposition of the servitude of access (page 175C). This then raised the question of whether a right of parking was a servitude known to the law. By the time the Appeal reached the House of Lords, the focus was on the primary issue, but it was also argued that, although a right accessory to a servitude does not need itself be capable of existing as a servitude, it is easier to accept the existence of such an accessory right if it can exist as a servitude in its own right.

These issues brought with them a number of sub-issues.

First was the basis upon which the claimed existence of, respectively, a servitude right or a right accessory to a servitude fell to be implied.

Second, whether a claimed right of parking was so extensive as to exclude the servient proprietor from exercising his rights of ownership over his property. Tied up in this was the difficult question of when stopping and unloading turns into parking and when parking turns into storage.

Third, arising from this was the question of whether a right of storage is a servitude recognised by the law.

It is proposed now to look at each of the Speeches in light of these questions.

The Speeches

Lord Hope of Craighead, concurring with Lord Neuberger of Abbotsbury, recorded (at paragraph [19]) that the respondents had conceded that the right of access included rights to turn vehicles and to load and unload both goods and passengers from them on land belonging to the third defender adjacent to the dominant tenement and went on (at paragraph [20]) to address the question whether a right to park is ever capable of being constituted as ancillary to an admitted servitude of vehicular access.

He stated, at paragraph [21] that it was hard to envisage a situation, other than where the right is constituted expressly by a feuing condition or as a real burden, where it would be necessary to rely on a servitude right to park on someone else's land which was not ancillary to a right of access over it in favour of the dominant tenement and continued, at paragraph [22]:

> "I doubt whether it is necessary for the purposes of this case to decide whether a right simply to park vehicles on someone else's land can be said to constitute a servitude in its own right, independently of a servitude right of way over that land by means of vehicles. So I would prefer to reserve my opinion on this point."

However, this was not his last word on the subject, as he went on to point out that the defenders had contended that it was not possible in the law of Scotland for there to be a servitude of parking.

He stated:

> "This point does indeed need to be addressed because, as my noble and learned friend Lord Neuberger of Abbotsbury points out, a right to park as an ancillary to a servitude of access would be difficult to accept if a right to park as a servitude in its own right was in principle unacceptable. It is on the objection in principle, therefore, on which a decision certainly is required in this case, that I wish to concentrate."

This he did by addressing the ouster argument (i.e. a right of parking would exclude the servient proprietor for his property), stating:

> "the fact that the servient proprietor is excluded from part of

> his property is not necessarily inimical to the existence of a servitude. I am not aware of any authority in Scotland which indicates the contrary. In principle therefore there seems to me to be no fundamental objection to the right which the pursuers seek to establish. I am fortified in this view by Lord Neuberger's valuable analysis of the English authorities."

Properly understood, then, Lord Hope accepted that there was no objection in principle to existence of a servitude of parking, and one might be constituted by express grant, but, the present case was one of an accessory right only since "it is obviously not possible to spell out of the words of the express grant in this case a self-standing servitude right to park vehicles on land belonging to the owner of the servient tenement." (paragraph [25]).

He then went on to draw the distinction that "a servitude... exists for the reasonable and comfortable enjoyment of the dominant tenement" (paragraph [26]) whereas, the question for ancillary rights is what rights "are necessary for the convenient and comfortable use and enjoyment *of the servitude.*" (paragraph [29]).

In judging this matter, consideration is not limited to those uses which were in existence of the time of the grant, but, rather, what uses were "in contemplation at the time of the grant, having regard to what the dominant proprietor might reasonably be expected to do in the exercise of his right to convenient and comfortable use of the property."

In dealing with the form of the Interlocutor, he stated at paragraph [39]:

> "As Lord Marnoch said in the Extra Division (para 24) questions of how and precisely where the right to park is to be exercised are questions that ought to be capable of being resolved by the parties acting sensibly but can, if necessary, be decided under reference to the rule that the servitude right must be used *civiliter*. This point has been recognised by the terms of the declarator, which refers to the right to park 'such

vehicles as are reasonably incidental to the enjoyment of said access to the dominant tenement.' The right is not to store or warehouse vehicles on the servient tenement. It is a right which is ancillary to the right of access to the dominant tenement. It is available only for the parking of vehicles which are intended to be used in the exercise of that right."

Lord Scott of Foscote started by expressing his view that there is "no difference relevant to any issue that arises in this case between the common law in England and Wales relating to easements and the common law in Scotland relating to servitudes." (paragraph [45]). He went on to say:

"The principle of civiliter, a Scottish law principle which regulates the manner in which a servitude may be exercised... is equally applicable, although not so named, under English law and requires the dominant owner, the owner entitled to exercise a servitudal right over the land of his neighbour, to exercise the right reasonably and without undue interference with the servient owner's enjoyment of his own land. The converse of this principle is that an interference by the servient owner with the dominant owner's exercise of the servitude will not be an actionable interference unless it prevents the dominant owner from making a reasonable use of the servitude....

"both the manner of exercise by the respondents of their rights over the servient land and the steps that could lawfully be taken by the appellants that might appear to interfere with those rights are subject to the principle of civiliter, a principle that, as it seems to me, limits the respondents' use of the servient land to a reasonable use but enables the appellants, subject only to an obligation not to interfere with that reasonable use, to make whatever use they wish of their servient land."

At paragraph [47], he stated:

> "In my opinion there should be no doubt that it is and, if there is any such doubt, that doubt should be now dispelled. I can see no reason in principle, subject to a few qualifications, why any right of limited use of the land of a neighbour that is of its nature of benefit to the dominant land and its owners from time to time should not be capable of being created as a servitudal right in rem appurtenant to the dominant land (see Gale, Easements, para 1.35). An essential qualification of the above stated proposition, a qualification that I would derive from the all-important civiliter principle, is that the right must be such that a reasonable use thereof by the owner of the dominant land would not be inconsistent with the beneficial ownership of the servient land by the servient owner."

He added, however, that, to the extent that the 'ouster' principle is asserting that a servitude must not be inconsistent with the continued beneficial ownership of the servient land by the servient owner, he would unreservedly accept it."

The Respondents had argued that the servitude right of vehicles was not a right accorded to vehicles, but to persons conveyed by vehicles, including the driver. This was picked up by Lord Scott at paragraph [52] that it was:

> "plain that the grant of a right to have vehicular access to Da Store must have contemplated that the vehicles by means of which access was obtained by those living at Da Store would have to be left parked at or near the Da Store gate until they were next needed and, accordingly, that a right of parking must accompany the right of vehicular access."

At paragraph [53] he looked at the question of where, precisely, on the servient tenement vehicles might be parked. He stated:

> "The principle of *civiliter* restricts the use that the dominant owners or their licensees can make of the servient land for parking their cars to a reasonable use for the purposes of Da Store as a domestic dwelling. In my opinion, the counterpart of that principle enables the servient owners to use their land, including the pink land, for their own purposes provided they do not interfere with the reasonable exercise by the dominant owners of their rights of access and parking. No one has suggested that the parking of two Da Store cars on the pink land is not a reasonable exercise of the parking right."

Against that background, he returned to consider the ouster principle, pointing out (at paragraph [54]) that every servitude or easement will bar some ordinary use of the servient land.

He then reviewed the relevant authorities. At paragraph [55], he considered the case of *Wright v Macadam* [1949] 2 KB 744 in which the Court of Appeal had decided that the right to use a coal shed could exist as an easement. He stated:

> "If the coal shed door had been locked with only the dominant owner possessing a key and entry by the servient owner barred, so that the dominant owner would have been in possession and control of the shed, I would have regarded it as arguable that the right granted was inconsistent with the servient owner's ownership and inconsistent with the nature of a servitude or an easement. But sole use for a limited purpose is not, in my opinion, inconsistent with the servient owner's retention of possession and control or inconsistent with the nature of an easement."

He concluded:

> [59] In my respectful opinion the test formulated in *London & Blenheim Estates Ltd v Ladbroke Retail Parks Ltd* and applied by the Court of Appeal in *Batchelor v Marlow*, a test

that would reject the claim to an easement if its exercise would leave the servient owner with no 'reasonable use' to which he could put the servient land, needs some qualification. It is impossible to assert that there would be no use that could be made by an owner of land over which he had granted parking rights. He could, for example, build above or under the parking area. He could place advertising hoardings on the walls. Other possible uses can be conjured up. And by what yardstick is it to be decided whether the residual uses of the servient land available to its owner are 'reasonable' or sufficient to save his ownership from being 'illusory'? It is not the uncertainty of the test that, in my opinion, is the main problem. It is the test itself. I do not see why a landowner should not grant rights of a servitudal character over his land to any extent that he wishes. The claim in *Batchelor v Marlow* for an easement to park cars was a prescriptive claim based on over 20 years of that use of the strip of land. There is no difference between the characteristics of an easement that can be acquired by grant and the characteristics of an easement that can be acquired by prescription. If an easement can be created by grant it can be acquired by prescription and I can think of no reason why, if an area of land can accommodate nine cars, the owner of the land should not grant an easement to park nine cars on the land. The servient owner would remain the owner of the land and in possession and control of it. The dominant owner would have the right to station up to nine cars there and, of course, to have access to his nine cars. How could it be said that the law would recognise an easement allowing the dominant owner to park five cars or six or seven or eight but not nine? I would, for my part, reject the test that asks whether the servient owner is left with any reasonable use of his land, and substitute for it a test which asks whether the servient owner retains possession and, subject to the reasonable exercise of the right in question, control of the servient land."

Lord Rodger of Earlsferry took a more robust view that his colleagues. He expressed the view that the correct test, in implying accessory rights, was not whether the rights were necessary for convenient and comfortable use and enjoyment, but whether they were "*essential*". This is a radically different, and stricter, test. He felt, in the circumstances of the case, that a right to park was not essential, but was reluctant to differ from the Sheriff, who had heard all the evidence and conducted a site inspection, so ended up concurring with the majority. (Paragraphs [83] and [97]).

However, despite his near-dissent on this matter, he was at one with his colleagues on the other matters of principle. In particular, on the question of whether a servitude of parking could exist in Scots Law, he concluded, at paragraph [75]:

> "Looking at the question as a matter of principle, like Lord Scott, I see no reason why a servitude of parking should not be recognised in Scots law."

At paragraph [76], he referred to the circumstance that a servitude of parking would involve a car being placed on the neighbour's land and this would prevent the neighbour using that part of his land when the car was stationed there, but said that this could not in itself be a conclusive objection to the existence of such a servitude since many well-known servitudes involve structures being erected or objects being placed on the servient land.

Lord Mance agreed with Lord Hope of Craighead that the correct test for implication of an accessory right was one of reasonably necessity for the enjoyment of the servitude. (paragraph [101]). He added, at paragraph [102]:

> "If, as I consider, a right to park can exist as impliedly ancillary to an express servitude right of access over property retained, I find it difficult to think that it cannot exist as an

> independent servitude over the property retained when this is impliedly necessary for the convenient and comfortable enjoyment of the property disposed of. However, it is not I think necessary for me to express a final view on this."

Lord Neuburger of Abbotsbury commented, at paragraphs [110] and [111], on the similarity of the Scots law of Servitudes and the English Law of Easements:

> "While some aspects of the juridical nature, origin and incidents of servitudes in Scotland are different from those of easements in England and Wales, there are many aspects of similarity... Servitudes and easements are inherently very similar, and there is very little difference between lifestyles and standards north and south of the Cheviots. Further, courts in both jurisdictions have expressly and beneficially relied on each other's analyses and developments in this area of law."

He affirmed "reasonable necessity" for "convenient and comfortable enjoyment" as the correct test for implication of a servitude or a right accessory to a servitude (paragraph [116]).

As to the number of vehicles which might be parked, he said that should be tested by what was in the presumed intention of the parties at the time of the grant, which would include the anticipated uses to which the land would be put. (Paragraphs [130] – [132]).

He then approached the question of principle – whether a parking could ever be a servitude – from the perspective of the ouster principle ([paragraph [134] *et seq.*) but, at paragraph [140] expressing the view that he was not satisfied that a right is prevented from being a servitude or an easement simply because the right granted would involve the servient owner being effectively excluded from the property. He referred to the decision of the Privy Council in *Attorney-General of Southern Nigeria v John Holt & Co (Liverpool) Ltd* (page 617) which, he said, appeared to have held that a right to store materials on land could be an easement although it involved the dominant owner enjoying an 'exclusive' right to enjoy the property concerned.

He concluded, at paragraph [143]:

> "Accordingly, I see considerable force in the views expressed by Lord Scott in his opinion (paras 57, 59) to the effect that a right can be an easement notwithstanding that the dominant owner effectively enjoys exclusive occupation, on the basis that the essential requirement is that the servient owner retains possession and control. If that were the right test, then it seems likely that *Batchelor v Marlow* was wrongly decided. However, unless it is necessary to decide the point to dispose of this appeal, I consider that it would be dangerous to try and identify degree of ouster is required to disqualify a right from constituting a servitude or easement, given the very limited argument your Lordships have received on the topic."

The Principles

From the above analysis, it is possible to identify a number of principles:

1. The law of servitudes in Scotland and the law of easements in England are substantially similar;

2. In principle, a right to park is capable of existing as servitude or easement in its own right.

3. Similarly a right to park can exist as a right accessory to a servitude or easement of access.

4. Such a servitude or servitude including an accessory right to park can be constituted by grant or by prescription.

5. In the case of implication of a servitude of parking, the test is what was in the reasonable contemplation of the parties at the time of the grant as being necessary for the reasonable and comfortable enjoyment of the dominant tenement (which would include the anticipated uses to which the land would be put.)

6. In the case of implication parking a right accessory to a servitude of access, the test is what was in the reasonable contemplation of the parties at the time of the grant as being necessary for the reasonable and comfortable enjoyment of the servitude.

7. In theory, the so-called ouster principle might defeat the establishment of a claimed servitude, but this is subject to the qualification that the correct test is whether the servient proprietor is deprived of possession and, subject to the reasonable exercise of the right in question, control of the servient tenement, and, in this context, the test formulated in *Batchelor v Marlow* as to whether the servient proprietor has any reasonable use of the servient tenement is not correct.

8. It is not necessary to specify the detailed manner in which the servitude can be exercised. Once the servitude has been established, it requires to be exercised *civiliter,*

This might all seem fairly clear, but there are areas where some litigants and legal writers have sought to kick back.

First, since the ground of decision was whether parking could exist as an accessory right, whatever was said about whether parking could be a servitude or easement in its own right was, strictly speaking *obiter*.

Second (it is often said), both Lord Hope and Lord Mance reserved their judgment on the question of principle as to whether parking could exist as a servitude in its own right, (though this ignores the context, explained above, in which Lord Hope expressed that comment).

In addition, from an English Law perspective, it is sometimes suggested that although the test in *Batchelor v Marlow* was strongly disapproved, that case was not over-ruled and still binds lower courts and that *Moncrieff v Jamieson*, being a Scottish case is merely persuasive and not binding.

These comments are technically correct, but, it might be suggested, rather miss the point as to the remarkable unanimity of view on the underlying common principles of Scots and English Law (*pace* Lord Rodger in relation to his dissenting view that the test for implication is "essential" rather than "necessary for reasonable and comfortable enjoyment").

Developments since Moncrieff v Jamieson

(a) Scotland

In Scotland, the first case to consider *Moncrieff* was *Holms v Ashfolds Estates Ltd* 2009 SLT 389.

In that case, title to a parking space was conveyed to purchasers of land, but, on taking possession they discovered that if a car were parked in the neighbouring space, it was impossible for them to drive into their own space. They sued the seller for a breach of the Warrandice in relation to the parking space. The court found that the principle of *caveat emptor* applied and the Warrandice did not cover the claimed disturbance of peaceful possession. In the course of submissions, reference had been made to the ouster principle.

In its judgment, the Extra Division stated, at paragraph [50]:

> In the course of the argument before us there was discussion of the so called "ouster" principle developed principally in the English cases relating to easements to which we were referred. In the event, we do not regard it as necessary for us

to embark upon an extensive examination of this particular area of the discussion. Servitude rights of vehicular access have long been recognised not only in Roman law and our law, but also in most legal systems. Naturally, the need to allow such access impedes the use to which the owner of the servient tenement may make of the land over which the access route lies. He may only make transient use of it while it is not required for access by the proprietor of the dominant tenement."

This adds little to the debate on exclusion of the servient proprietor, though perhaps the Court was unnecessarily dismissive of the ouster principle, for, though the terminology might be English, as *Moncrieff* shows, the underlying principle is equally applicable in Scots Law.

Of perhaps greater import was *Johnson Thomas & Thomas and Others v Smith and Others* [2016] SC GLA 50 which directly addressed the questions of principle raised on *Moncrieff*. In this case, the pursuers sought a Declarator that the second defender's property was the servient tenement in a servitude of parking in which the pursuer's property was the dominant tenement. The defenders challenged this. They denied that there did exist a free-standing servitude of parking; they stated that in any event the servitude claimed was repugnant with the second defender's ownership; they complained that the declarator sought did not specify the number and identity of persons and vehicles likely to be exercising the supposed right.

The Sheriff (S. Reid) approached the first objection by considering the historical development of the law of servitudes, challenging the belief (supported by the Scottish Law Commission in its *Report on Real Burdens*, referred to above, that there was a "fixed list" of servitudes, then (at paragraph [29]) he turned to consider whether there existed a servitude of parking. He considered the speeches in Moncrieff, acknowledging that the comments on the existence of a free-standing servitude of parking were, strictly speaking, *obiter,* but adding that:

65

> "the preponderance of opinion was plainly that such a right can competently exist in Scots law; and it seems to me that the dicta to that effect are so intimately bound up with the strict ratio of the case, that at times the border between *ratio decidendi* and mere *obiter dicta* becomes well nigh indistinguishable."

He concluded, at paragraph [33]:

> "In summary, while I acknowledge that *Moncrieff* does not represent a strictly binding judicial recognition of the existence of a free-standing servitude right, in my judgment the debate on this narrow issue is ended for all practical purposes by the overwhelming current of eminent *obiter dicta* in that case. It is futile to stand Canute-like against it. From *Moncrieff*, it is but a short skip in logic to conclude, by analogy with the ancillary right recognised in that case, that an independent free-standing servitude right is, at least, similar in nature thereto."

Referring to Lord Roger at paragraph [75] in *Moncrieff* and Lord President Emslie in *Irvine Knitters Ltd v North Ayrshire Cooperative Society Ltd* 1978 SLT 105 at page 109, [which case is also reported at 1978 SC 109] the Sheriff observed at paragraph [35] that any servitude can be exercised only for the benefit of the dominant tenement and for the lawful purposes to which the dominant tenement can be put. He acknowledged that a servitude of parking could be constituted by prescription as well as by express grant, but, in looking at the extent of use over the prescriptive period, any evidence of use which was not for a lawful purpose to which the dominant tenement could be put would be irrelevant.

He then went on to consider the defenders' submission that the supposed servitude was repugnant with their ownership of the land because the exercise of the supposed right could result in the entire area of the servient tenement being covered by vehicles, every day and all day, thereby excluding the proprietor from any practical or realistic enjoyment or use of the land.

This, he said (at paragraph [41]) was a supposed principle which was not engaged:

> "The partial or total exclusion of the second defender from mere physical occupation of the servient tenement does not of itself prevent the asserted right from being a servitude."

He then considered the judgments in *Moncreiff*, and referred to Lord Scott's proposed test of "possession and control" rather than the test of "reasonable use". He stated, at paragraph [44]:

> "For my own part, I see much force in Lord Scott's reasoned articulation of the repugnancy principle. A servitude right of parking may well substantially restrict the rights of the owner of the servient tenement and the uses to which, from time to time, he can put the surface of the land, but his rights as proprietor are not sterilised. He can build over the servient tenement, he can build under it, he can advertise on hoardings around it, or otherwise utilise the boundary walls. Indeed, he can park on it himself, or use it for any other purpose, provided he does not interfere to any material extent with the reasonable exercise of the servitude right by the dominant proprietor. The servient proprietor may not have physical occupation of the surface of the land when the servitude right is being exercised, but he remains the owner of the land, he remains in control of it, he remains in (legal) possession of it, and he is at liberty to exploit its residual uses."

The Sheriff then went on to deal with the defender's criticism of alleged lack of specification in the declarator which was sought, noting that "it was submitted that the declaratory crave fails to specify essential matters such as the number and type of vehicles that can be parked on the land; where on the land they can be parked; and when, by whom, and for how long they can be parked there."

He rejected that criticism. He referred to the dictum of Lord President Clyde in *Carstairs v Spence* 1924 SC 380 that prescriptive use not merely establishes the existence of a servitude right but, in some most important ways, defines the extent of the right. However, he explained that the reference to "extent" was a reference to the form of the right – for example, in the case of a right of access, whether it is pedestrian, equine or vehicular. Once a type or category of servitude is constituted by reference to the prescriptive use, including, in the case of a servitude right of access, its particular form, there is no need to further specify its use.

He concluded (paragraph [54]):

> "It is not necessary, in the context of a crave for declarator of a servitude right of vehicular parking constituted by prescriptive possession, to specify the precise (or maximum) number, type or model of vehicles to be parked on the servient tenement; or where on the land they can be parked; or when, by whom, and for how long they can be parked there."

Indeed, he went on to caution about the confusion which could be caused by over-specifying the right, and pointed out that, in *Moncrieff* the Declarator which was sought had originally specified a precise number of vehicles, but had been amended before the Inner House to remove that specification.

The Sheriff then went on to deal head-on with a matter which had only been touched on in *Moncrieff*: stopping, parking and storage.

At paragraph [61] he stated:

> "In my judgment, a servitude right of vehicular parking, by its nature, comprises the right to station a vehicle temporarily upon the servient tenement. The component elements of

> this definition may give rise to factual subtleties and questions of degree, varying from case to case. A vehicle is a moveable conveyance. The temporary or transitory nature of its presence on the servient tenement distinguishes the activity from permanent storage. But the parking need not be brief. A vehicle may quite legitimately be parked for a few minutes or hours, or for a much longer period of days, weeks or many months *(Moncrieff v Jamieson* 2005 SC 281 at 289 per Lord Marnoch). It is only if, in nature, the supposed "parking" constitutes at inception (or evolves into) permanent storage or deposit, then such an activity would not be justified by the servitude right (*Moncrieff*, supra, at paragraph [39] per Lord Hope).

Although this was a decision at first instance in the Sheriff Court which has not been reported, the authority of its logic is clear and convincing. It has been relied upon in at least one other case (*McCabe v Paterson* [2020] SC GLA 14) and, although there has since been a number of cases in Scotland concerning claimed servitudes of parking, it would appear that the very existence of that servitude has not been challenged in any of those cases.

The next significant case was *Johnston v Davidson* 2021 SC (SAC) 9, an appeal in the Sheriff Appeal Court. In that case, the pursuer's title contained an express grant of a servitude right "of access." He could drive to a point a short distance from his house, but required to go the rest of the way on foot. He sought a declarator that he had a right of vehicular access to his property over the adjacent property with an ancillary right to park vehicles on the alleged servient tenement. In finding that there was a right of vehicular access and an accessory right to park, the Sheriff said he did so by looking at both issues together, "holistically". Although the Sheriff Appeal Court supported the Sheriff's conclusion, it criticised the Sheriff's approach. Instead, it laid down what it described as a two-stage approach:

> "First, to determine the nature of the right conferred by the express grant; and having done so, to determine what ancillary rights were necessary for the comfortable enjoyment of the servitude." (Paragraph [24]).

Following that process, the Sheriff Appeal Court found that the right conferred by the express grant was, in the circumstances, one of vehicular access and that the claimed ancillary right of parking was necessary for the comfortable use and enjoyment of the servitude.

This two-stage approach was explicitly approved in the later Sheriff Appeal Court case of *Macallan v Arbuckle* (No. 3) [2022] SAC (Civ) 9.

The case of *McCabe v Paterson* [2022] (Civ) 2(Civ) concerned not a right to park as an ancillary right to a right of vehicular access, but a claimed ancillary right to lock a gate which was situated on the access road over the servient tenement, as a means of securing the yard which was the dominant tenement.

The Sheriff had found that there could not be an accessory right of gate locking as such a right could not exist as a standalone servitude, and that, in any event, the locking of the gate deprived the servient proprietor of his ownership.

On the first point, the parties both acknowledged (and the Sheriff Appeal Court agreed) that a claimed accessory right does not require to be capable of existing as a servitude in its own right, and, accordingly, the Sheriff was in error in this respect.

On the deprivation of ownership point, the Appellant argued that it commonly happens that a servient proprietor may place and lock an access gate on an access road, but this is acceptable so long as the servient proprietor provides the dominant proprietor with a key. The speciality in the present case was that it was the proprietor of the dominant tenement who had locked the gate and provided the proprietor of the servient tenement with a key. In this regard, the Appellant referred to the comment of Lord Scott in *Moncreiff* at paragraph [55] that it would be a deprivation of ownership if a dominant proprietor locked a coalshed *and did not provide the servient proprietor with a key*. The Appellant also referred to a Scottish case, *Magistrates of Glasgow v Bell* (1776), in which the court had found that a servient proprietor was permitted to lock a gate so long as he provided the dominant proprietor with a key and two English cases which had determined that the locking of a gate did not constitute adverse possession (*Littledale v Liverpool College* [1900] 1CH 19 and Amirtharaja v White [2021] EWHC 330 (Ch)).

The Court accepted that the correct test was possession and control (at paragraph [76]), but found that there was, indeed, repugnancy. Dealing with the Appellant's arguments, the court declined to follow *Magistrates of Glasgow v Bell* on the basis that it accepted the criticism made of it in *Cusine and Paisley* at paragraph 12.98 that it is no longer good law, and distinguished the English cases primarily on the basis that they concerned adverse possession, which, according to the SAC required rather more than possession and control. Further, Lord Scott's comment in *Moncrieff* was "a fragile basis for asserting the right of the dominant tenement to erect and lock a gate" (paragraph [82]) and "was not part of his judicial determination, but a prelude to his own consideration of the facts as found by the sheriff in *Moncrieff*" (paragraph [91].

This analysis is open to criticism in a number of respects, and it is unclear whether another court would reach the same view should a similar case arise in future, but the case was probably not wrongly decided, because the court's subsidiary reason for rejecting the appeal was that the claimed accessory right may have been necessary for reasonable and comfortable enjoyment of the dominant tenement, but not (which was the correct test) for the reasonable and comfortable enjoyment of the *servitude*.

In the case of *Doolan v Donald [2024]* SC LIV 15, the pursuer, who was the proprietor of a dominant tenement which enjoyed a servitude right of access over a driveway, sought interdict against the proprietor of the servient tenement from parking on the driveway. Her proposition was:

71

> "That the Pursuers must be free to use any part of the access driveway at any time and the presence of parked vehicles denies them that freedom; they should not have to navigate any items on the driveway in order to exercise their Servitude Right; and there is no right for either party to park on the shared driveway area."

It is scarcely surprising that the court rejected that proposition.

(b) England

The first reported case in England to consider Moncrieff was *Virdi v Chana* [2008] EWHC 2901(Ch). This concerned a claimed easement of parking acquired by prescription. The core argument was whether a right of parking could exist as a separate easement. The Adjudicator (from whose decision the Appeal was taken) was that *Batchelor v Marlow* was no longer good law, and that the correct test was control and possession as suggested by Lord Scott in *Moncrieff*.

The judge stated (at paragraph [24]):

> "I would agree with this approach, which seems compelling as a matter of first principle, were it open to me to do so. It seems to me, however, that despite the support that this approach has from the House of Lords in *Moncrieff*, in particular from the helpful article of Mr Alexander Hill-Smith to which Lord Scott paid tribute at paragraph [61], the observations of their Lordships were strictly *obiter* on this point. As *Batchelor v Marlow* was not overruled, I should continue to regard myself as bound by the Court of Appeal's decision in that case."

However, even applying the "deprivation of reasonable use" case, he agreed with the adjudicator that, on the facts of the case, the servient proprietor was not deprived of reasonable use of her property since she could still use the servient property by maintaining it, dealing with it as owner. For example: "she can grow a plant or trellis close to the fence (so long as it does not prevent parking); she could place bicycles on this land; she could alter the surface, replace and repaint the fencing, and so on."

The first consideration of *Moncrieff* by the Court of Appeal was in *Waterman v Boyle* [2009] EWCA Civ 116.

The judge at first instance had held that an ancillary right to park on a driveway fell to be implied in the particular servitude right of vehicular access in that case. The Court of Appeal rejected that finding. It explained that the test to be applied was whether, having regard to the circumstances at the time of the original transfer it would have been a reasonably necessary use of the servient tenement to use it for stationing vehicles for the duration of the user's visit to the property. It was not enough that the use was merely desirable.

The court stated (at paragraph [34]):

> *Moncrieff* provides no support for the judge's conclusion. That case established that for the purposes of Scots law (which for this purpose was held to be the same as English law: see [29], [45] and [111]) a right to park was capable of being implied into a right of vehicular access if the right to park was reasonably necessary for the exercise or enjoyment of that right. On the facts of that case, the test for the implication of the right to park was met. But the facts were quite exceptional... The facts of Moncrieff are far removed from the present case, and the case turned on its special facts. The test applied in that case is that set out above but its application to the facts of this case leads to a very different result."

It is to be noted that, since this case involved accessory rights, the question of whether there was a servitude of parking, and the correctness of the decision in *Batchelor v Marlow* did not arise.

In *Parshall v Bryans* [2012] EWHC 665 (Ch), a case which concerned the registration of a claimed servitude of parking, both counsel agreed that such a servitude might exist. The Court was obliged to proceed upon that basis, but the judge said (at paragraph [25]):

> "The easement sought by the Respondents would in practical effect amount to a right of user of the land to the exclusion of the Appellants. Whether that is capable as a matter of law of constituting an easement has been a matter of acute debate in recent times, but, though receiving support from recent *obiter* observations by members of the Supreme Court in *Moncrieff v Jamieson* [2007] 1 WLR 2620, remains undecided. Since Counsel for the Appellants told me that he did not dispute that the law could in principle recognize such an easement, I heard no submissions on that proposition. While the Appellants may of course concede whatever they wish affecting relations with their neighbours, I would have had significant reservations about ordering the alteration of the register to include as an easement an arrangement which may not amount to one as a matter of law, merely because the servient owner does not contest the proposition."

However, shortly afterwards, the Court did directly address this matter in *Kettel v Bloomfold Ltd.* [2012] EWHC 1422 (Ch). In that case, the Claimants were leaseholders of eight flats in a development of which the defendants were the Freeholders. Each flat had the use of a designated parking space. The Claimants sought an injunction to prevent the defendants from building over the parking spaces. The first issue considered by the court was whether the grant was a demise or an easement. On construing the terms of the grant, the Court noted that each tenant was not granted "sole use" of the car parking space, but rather the sole right to use it for parking and that this was not the language of exclusive possession, so was not a demise.

Both counsel had accepted that it was possible for a right to park to exist as an easement. At paragraph [11], the Court referred to Lord Scott's criticism of the test in *Batchelor v Marlow,* but stated (at paragraph [12]) that *Batchelor v Marlow* had not been overruled and remained binding on him. However he also referred specifically to *Virdi v Chana* and then proceeded to consider the facts in the present case in the light of the "deprivation of reasonable use" test.

He stated, at paragraph [21]:

> "There is no doubt that an easement for parking can exist, but it seems to me that notwithstanding the agreement between counsel I must address the question whether I am precluded by *Batchelor v Marlow* from finding that an easement exists in this case."

He concluded that the rights exercisable by the defendant over the space could not be said in the circumstances of the case to leave him with no reasonable use of the land and so make his ownership of it illusory. At paragraph [23], he pointed out that the defendant could do anything that a freeholder could normally do, except to the extent that it would be inconsistent with the express right to park a car, together with any terms to be implied as a normal matter of construction:

> "Thus the defendant may pass on foot or by vehicle across the space freely if there is no vehicle parked on it for the time being or avoiding one that is. He may authorise others to do likewise (and has done so in the other estate leases). He may choose, change and repair the surface, keep it clean and remove obstructions (and is obliged to do so in providing the Services). He may lay pipes or other service media under it, as he may wish to do for the benefit of the estate buildings. He may in principle build above it... or provide overhead projections such as wires."

Next, in the case of *Begley v Taylor* [2014] EWHC 1180 (Ch) the court declared (at paragraph [81]) that, under reference to *Moncrieff*, "It is now clear that a right to park is capable of being an easement and that such an easement can be acquired by prescription." Comment was made as to the criticism of *Bachelor v Marlow* in *Moncrieff*, but the judge pointed out that it had not been over-ruled and therefore it was binding on him. He then analysed each of the claimed rights of parking and concluded that, on the facts of the case, the owner of the servient tenement was not deprived of reasonable use of his land.

De la Cuona v Big Apple Marketing Ltd. [2017] EWHC 3783 (Ch) was the next case to address the ouster principle. The judge referred to the criticism of *Batchelor v Marlow*, "not least" from the House of Lords in *Moncrieff*, but acknowledged that, as had been recognised by judges in other cases, *Batchelor v Marlow* remained binding on English first instance judges, and he had to proceed on that basis. He added, however (at paragraph [15]) that *Batchelor v Marlow* had not, however, prevented the validity of rights to park being upheld in several cases in recent years. He referred specifically to *Virdi*, *Begley* and *Kettle*.

He then went on at paragraphs [21] to [24] to review the facts of the case and agreed with the judge at first instance who had found that:

> "the grantor retains reasonable use of the Allocated Spaces once designated and his right to use them is not illusory. Whilst the grantor does covenant not to interfere with the grantee's right to park and so on, that does not mean that the grantor cannot use them when the grantee is not there, cannot walk over them when the grantee is not there, cannot perhaps allow other people to do so."

(c) The Principles revisited

If one revisits the principles derived from *Moncreiff v Jamieson* in the list of the above developments, the following further additional conclusions can be drawn:

1. There can now be no doubt that the law of Scotland and the Law of England both recognise the existence of a servitude of parking and of a right of parking, where appropriate, as an accessory to a right of access.

2. The Law of Scotland has no difficulty in applying the correct test of ouster or repugnancy, namely Lord Scott's test of whether the servient proprietor is deprived of possession and control of the servient tenement.

3. In English law, until such time as *Bachelor v Marlowe* comes to be over-ruled, the courts are constrained by *stare decisis* to apply the *Bachelor v Marlow* test of whether the servient owner is left with no 'reasonable use' to which he could put the servient land.

4. However, whereas the *Batchelor v Marlowe* test was originally articulated as a reasoned objection to the possibility of a servitude of parking existing at all, it has now been distinguished to the effect of becoming only an objection to a particular claimed servitude of parking which might be claimed to exist in a particular case.

5. Given that the English courts have tended to find that almost any residual use of the servient tenement is a "reasonable use", it is very difficult to conceive of a situation in practice in which the *Batchelor* test will be found to have been met.

6. Consequently, notwithstanding the important theoretical difference between Scotland and England, for practical purposes the outcome in both jurisdictions in any given case is likely to be

the same.

Practical issues can arise as to the manner of exercise of servitude rights of parking, but, since these practical questions are similar to those arising in relation to other parking rights, discussion of these issues will be postponed until after consideration of other parking rights.

CHAPTER FOUR

SERVITUDES AND REAL BURDENS IN SCOTLAND IN TERMS OF THE TITLE CONDITIONS (SCOTLAND) ACT 2003

As noted above, the Scottish Law Commission, having reached the (in retrospect, erroneous) view that the list of servitudes was closed, made certain recommendations for reform of the law of servitudes, which were given effect to in part 7 of the *Title Conditions (Scotland) Act 2003*

Section 75(1) of the Act provided:

> "75 *Creation of positive servitude by writing: deed to be registered*
>
> (1) A deed is not effective to create a positive servitude by express provision unless it is registered against both the benefited property and the burdened property."

and section 76 provided:

> "76 *Disapplication of requirement that positive servitude created in writing be of a known type*
>
> (1) Any rule of law that requires that a positive servitude be of a type known to the law shall not apply in relation to any servitude created in accordance with section 75(1) of this Act.

> (2) Nothing in subsection (1) above permits the creation of a servitude that is repugnant with ownership."

Section 79 made it incompetent to create negative real burdens from the date on which the Act came into force, and section 80 made provision for the conversion of negative servitudes into real burdens.

So far as parking is concerned, it was supposed that, on the basis that parking was not a servitude known to the law of Scotland, servitudes of parking would, for the first time, be permitted to be created by registration under section 75(1), and that there would not exist any other forms of the servitude of parking.

However, given that the law does recognise servitudes of parking, then the following means of creation exist:

1. Express grant by deed granted prior to 28th November, 2004 (the day upon which Part 7 came into force);

2. Express grant by deed after 28th November, 2004 and registration under the Act;

3. Implied grant or reservation;

4. Prescription, whensoever arising.

An attempt was made in *Johnson, Thomas and Thomas* to argue that the claimed servitude was contrary to section 76(2) as being "repugnant with ownership."

However, the court found (at paragraph [20]) that the Act was not engaged, pointing out that:

> "Implied servitudes, or servitudes said to be constituted by prescription, remain unaffected by the statutory disapplication of the common law principle."

and, further in any event, that a servitude of parking was not "repugnant with ownership".

In theory, it might at least theoretically be possible to create a right to park as a real burden, but it will be noted that section 81 of the Act provides:

> "81 *Certain real burdens to become positive servitudes*
>
> (1) A real burden consisting of a right to enter, or otherwise make use of, the burdened property shall, on the appointed day, cease to exist as such but shall forthwith become a positive servitude."

The Scottish Law Commission explained at paragraphs 12.2 and 12.15 of its Report that any such rights constituted as real burdens should be converted into servitudes.

Further Principle:

To the principles listed above, therefore, can be added the principle that the common law of servitudes of parking remains unaffected save only to the extent that new servitudes of parking which are to be created by deed can be so created after 28th November, 2004, only by the mechanism provided in the 2004 Act.

CHAPTER FIVE

PARKING UNDER LEASES AND OTHER RIGHTS

Of course, it is always possible for rights to park to be obtained in other ways. For example, the owner of land may grant a personal licence to his neighbours or others to park on that land; there may grow up a custom of the neighbours parking on the land without objection from the owner of the land, and, if that occurs, that may or may not give rise to a mere liberty, or to a personal right against the owner of the land, whether or not founded upon estoppel (or, in Scotland personal bar, whether by acquiescence or otherwise); and, of course, there may be contained in a Lease a clause which confers a right to park upon a lessee or tenant. In the last-mentioned event, the terms of the grant lease will require to be interpreted. The first question to be asked is whether there is a lease of the parking space itself, or merely the granting of a right to park in either a defined parking space or more generally in a wider area.

In interpreting the terms of the grant, there can be an issue as to whether that right is in reality a right under a lease, or a servitude, or a mere licence. All will depend on the interpretation of the terms of the grant.

The sort of quite nuanced issues which can arise are exemplified in the case of *Duchess of Bedford House RTM Co Ltd v Campden Hill Gate Ltd* [2023] R.T.R. 16. That case involved the question of whether certain claimed parking rights were reserved to the Lessor in terms of a 1969 headlease, and, if so, whether they fell within a reservation from rights conveyed in a subsequent lease granted by the Lessor in 1974. Central to that question was the nature of the right.

The relevant facts were that there was a block of flats situated on a private road which led to a square which was in the ownership of the Lessor. At the time of the grant of the 1969 lease there was a practice of the leaseholders parking in that square. In light of that, the judge at first instance had found that a right to park on the private road appurtenant to the block had existed in 1969. He further found that right had been reserved to the freeholder by the 1969 headlease, the effect of which was to convert what had previously been only a *de facto* right or quasi-easement into a legal easement.

On appeal, one of the issues was whether the judge was correct in finding that the parking right had become an easement. There were 47 flats in the block but room only for 20 to 22 vehicles in the square. The appellant argued that the claimed right to park could not be an easement as it was too diffuse and general in extent, and, further and in any event (under reference to *Moncrieff*) potentially of such a broad scope that it went beyond the form of parking easement recognised as valid in the authorities, which typically involves a right to park a vehicle or a number of vehicles in a defined area.

This argument was rejected by the Court. The judge stated, at paragraph [76]:

> "I do not regard the right as too vague or diffuse. The real nub of the objection seems to be that, on any view of it, there were an insufficient number of car parking spaces on Sheldrake Place East to accommodate each and every one of the occupants of Duchess of Bedford House, if they all chose to try and park at the same time. That does not appear to me to be a valid objection, however. The claimed right was not a right to park exercisable come what may, but only a right exercisable in competition with others."

A yet further issue which can arise is where parking is claimed on the basis of an ownership right – whether that be joint property, common property or common interest. The answer in any given case will be fact-driven and dependant on the rules of the property regime in question, so it is not proposed to deal with those issues here.

CHAPTER SIX

THE EXERCISE OF THE PRIVATE PARKING RIGHTS

However they may be constituted, problems arise in the exercise of parking rights.

In the case of servitudes there are certain obligations for their exercise which are implied by law. These were explained by Lord Jauncey of Tullichettle, (with whom the other judges concurred) in the House of Lords in the case of *Alvis v Harrison* 1991 SLT 64. In that case, the pursuer owned a castle which was approached by a driveway. The defender was the proprietor of an adjacent area of ground. He had, in his favour, an express grant of a servitude right of access over the driveway, including the verge. He created a new access road on his own land to enable him to access a public road with a bellmouth which he also created, but which encroached on the verge of the castle driveway. The pursuer succeeded at first instance and on appeal to the Inner House with his claim for damages for encroachment on the verge.

The defender successfully appealed to the House of Lords. Lord Jauncey (at page 67I to 68C) set out the following principles:

1. "Where a right of access is granted in general terms the owner of the dominant tenant is entitled to exercise that right not only for the purpose of the use to which the tenement is then being put but also for any other lawful purposes to which it may be put thereafter." (67I)

2. "The right must be exercised *civiliter*, that is to say,

reasonably and in a manner least burdensome to the servient tenement. As it is put in Rankine, Land-ownership in Scotland (4th ed.), p. 417: "It must be exercised in the mode least disadvantageous to the servient tenement, consistently with full enjoyment." (67L)

3. "For the better enjoyment of his right the dominant owner may improve the ground over which that right extends provided that he does not substantially alter the nature of the road nor otherwise prejudice the servient tenement". (*ibid*)

4. "A servitude right of access enures to the benefit of the dominant tenement and no other. Thus it cannot be communicated for the benefit of other tenements contiguous thereto" (68A).

The appeal succeeded as the House took the view that the Inner House had mistakenly applied principles which were appropriate to a right of access acquired by prescriptive possession rather than to a right acquired by express grant, and, that further, interpreting the words of the grant, the defender had been entitled to do what he had done.

Lord Jauncey noted that the position in England was similar.

It is worth underlining, in relation to the second principle, that the *civiliter* requirement may not be used to cut down the extent of a servitude. It is concerned with the manner of the exercise of a servitude right, not with the prior question of the extent of the right (*Moncrieff v Jamieson* per Lord Rodger of Earlsferry at paragraph [95] and *Lothian Amusements Ltd v The Kilns Developments Ltd* [2019] CSOH 51 at paragraph [52].

The counterpart of the above principles is that the owner of the servient tenement may make use of his property as he chooses, provided he respects the servitude right and causes no material interference with, or material obstruction to, its proper exercise.

These principles are of general application (though, as it happened, *Alvis* concerned a servitude of access) and one can see how these principles might come into play in a parking case.

Take, for example, a servient tenement on which is situated a car park which is used by staff, suppliers and customers while they visit a shop which is situated on the dominant tenement. The owner of the dominant tenement then buys an adjacent plot of land, which he holds on a separate title. He demolishes the buildings on both plots, builds, on the combined plot, a large supermarket, and then uses the car park for visitors to the new supermarket. Is this permissible?

The first question would be whether the servitude was constituted by express grant (in which case the court would require to construe the grant – as in *Alvis* above – or implied grant, in which case the court would require to determine the extent of the grant by looking at what was in the reasonable contemplation of the parties as to the future use of the dominant tenement (as in *Moncrieff*), or by prescription, where the badge of the right would be the extent of possession.

Next, there comes into play the first of the principles mentioned by Lord Jauncey, that the dominant proprietor can put his property to any lawful use.

The present example is not entirely invented, as it is what actually happened in the case of *Irvine Knitters Ltd. v. North Ayrshire Cooperative Society Ltd* 1978 S.C. 109. (albeit that the right in question was access, rather than parking). In that case, Lord Cameron said (at page 121):

> "In the deed of constitution of this servitude there is nothing which places any limit on the purposes to which the subjects may be put, and therefore it can be said that not only is there no limit on the extent of user but also no limit on the purpose which the proprietors of the dominant tenement as

such proprietors may lawfully pursue within the subjects or for which they may use them."

Let us say that the dominant tenement was a house, rather than a shop, and the title contained a prohibition on the property being used for anything other than residential purposes. In that event, the use of the dominant tenement for retail purposes would not be a lawful use, and so, the servitude could not be used to allow the car park to be used for the supermarket.

However, suppose that (as in *Irvine Knitters*) there was no such restriction, then the first principle might look as though it gives *carte blanche* to the dominant proprietor to increase the user on the servient tenement.

However, what would then come into play (and what did in fact come in to play in *Irvine Knitters*) would be the fourth principle: the servitude exists for the benefit of the first plot of land, but not the second, so using the car park for the benefit of the combined land (even though in the same ownership) was not permissible.

Suppose, however, that the dominant tenement had been a single plot of land, and that two small shops had been replaced by a large shopping mall.

In that event, the first condition would have been satisfied and the fourth would not have applied. However, the issue would then be whether there had been an unlawful increase in the burden beyond what was reasonably contemplated. That is a matter which is heavily fact-dependant and can be a matter of degree. For example, by analogy with *Keith v Texaco Ltd* 1977 SLT (Lands Tr.) 16 (where a right of access to a single house and garage was used for access to a housing estate) a similar increase in user for a car park serving the house than being used to serve a housing estate would clearly be an impermissible increase in the burden, but whether or not that would also be the case with a shop being replaced by a shopping mall, or a shop being replaced a supermarket may not be as clear.

Suppose that the use of a car park to serve the new supermarket is found not to be an impermissible increase in the burden, but, suppose also that the dominant proprietor then begins to operate it as a public car park, charging members of the public (rather than only visitors to the supermarket) to park there. Although there might well be an argument that allowing public parking would constitute an impermissible increase in the burden, that argument would be likely to be academic, as such user certainly would be impermissible for the reason that the car park would not then being used only for the purposes of the dominant tenement.

Suppose that the servient proprietor surfaces a previously unsurfaced parking area. Arguably, the third principle could be used to justify this, but it plainly would not justify building a multi-storey car park. Indeed, such an extreme example would raise acutely the question of whether the servient proprietor had been deprived of possession and control of his property.

It would be possible to go on multiplying examples, but the point is that any practical issue regarding the use of a servitude of parking which may arise should be capable of being analysed on the basis of the principles noted above.

> 5. The counterpart of the above principles is that the owner of the servient tenement may make use of his property as he chooses, provided he respects the servitude right and causes no material interference with, or material obstruction to, its proper exercise.

The question is whether this extends to changes in the manner of exercise of the servitude right over the property. Of course, such changes can always be agreed between the dominant and servient proprietor, (as, for example, happened with the changing of the line of the access road in *Moncrieff*), but issues can arise where the servient proprietor purports to impose changes unilaterally.

This specific question arose in the case of *Kettel v Bloomfold Ltd*. [2012]

EWHC 1422 (Ch), discussed above. The judge (H. H. Judge David Cooke) dealt with the question starting at paragraph [32]. He stated (at paragraph [33]):

> "In general, a servient landowner has no right unilaterally to extinguish an easement over one area of land on provision of an equivalent easement over another—see *Greenwich Healthcare NHS Trust v London and Quadrant Housing Trust* [1998] 1 W.L.R. 1749 — and I held in *Heslop v Bishton* [2009] EWHC 607 (Ch) that obstruction of the easement originally granted did not cease to be actionable in principle because of the availability of an alternative easement, even if equally convenient."

However, he added:

> "An easement may of course be granted in terms which, expressly or by implication permit variation of the servient land... but [in this case] there is no right of variation expressly set out and no basis, in my judgment, for such a right to be implied."

Assuming, however, there is a provision which might potentially be applicable, the court will require first, to construe that provision, and then to determine whether, in light of the particular circumstances, whether it does give the servient proprietor the latitude claimed. Furthermore, although the present discussion proceeds from the perspective of servitude rights, it will readily be appreciated that similar considerations may arise when considering rights conferred under a lease.

This is illustrated by the case of *Saeed v Plustrade* (*cit. supra*). As noted above, the circumstances were that a tenant was granted a right under her lease along with other tenants "to park on such part of the retained property as may from time to time be specified by the lessor as reserved for car parking, subject to such regulations as the lessor may make from time to time." She and the other tenants parked on an area which had been designated for parking and which had 13 spaces available. However, purporting to rely upon that provision in the Lease, the Lessor then blocked off that area to prevent anyone from parking there, offering, in substitution, an alternative area which had only 4 spaces available.

The court approached this first by construing the terms of the grant contained in the lease. This being an exercise in construction of the *terms* of the grant, it was not necessary, as the judge pointed out, to determine the *nature* of the grant – whether lease or easement.

The judge determined that, on a proper construction of the grant, the right which was conferred was not determinable at the whim of the Lessor. He continued at paragraphs [38] and [39]):

> "The defendants have undeniably interfered with the exercise of that right, by purporting to specify a new and much reduced specified area as from August 1, 2000 and by indicating their intention to restrict further use of the forecourt by the claimant for parking accordingly. To succeed in her claim under this head, however, she has to show that the interference with the exercise of her right has been substantial.
>
> "It is well established that the owner of an easement cannot complain of an interference with the exercise of such right unless it is both unjustified and "substantial" (see *Petty v. Parsons* [1914] 2 Ch. 653 and *Overcom Properties v. Stockleigh Hall Residents Management Ltd* (1988) 58 P. & C.R. 1). Even if the claimant's right to park does not qualify as an easement, she can in my judgment complain of the present interference on the ground of derogation from grant if, though only if, the interference is substantial. So the test is the same."

At paragraph [41], he concluded:

"Before the interference, the claimant was able to park on some 12 or 13 spaces in competition with a number of other persons. At that point she was restricted to parking on three or four spaces in competition with the same number of persons. This must constitute substantial interference with the enjoyment of her right."

Therefore, he found the interference unlawful as being a substantial derogation from the grant.

It will be recollected that the reasoning process and outcome in the later case of *Duchess of Bedford House RTM Co Ltd v Campden Hill Gate Ltd* (cit. supra) was similar.

Shah v Colvia Management Co. Ltd. [2008] EWCA Civ 19 was a case where what was in issue was parking rights under a lease, rather than in the form of a servitude. In that case, there was an industrial estate in which the parking area was inadequate for the number of tenants, although the leases granted each tenant:

"the full right and liberty for the Tenant and all persons authorised by him (in common with all other persons entitled to the like right) to use the car parks on the Estate and the amenity land on the Estate for the purpose from time to time allocated by the Company and subject to such reasonable rules and regulations for the common enjoyment thereof as the Company may from time to time prescribe."

As with the cases discussed above, the right was, effectively, a right to compete with the other tenants to find a parking space.

To deal with this, the defendant, Colvia Management Ltd., promulgated a scheme which banned overnight parking save on payment of a fee. The Claimants maintained that the rules and regulation of the scheme were reasonable and sought that they be set aside. The Court of Appeal determined that the scheme was reasonable. Its decision case very much depended on the particular facts, but the Court did give some general guidance which could be applicable in other cases.

First, the parking was managed by a separate management company, rather than the Lessor. Delivering the leading judgment, Lloyd LJ stated, at paragraph [21]:

> "Provisions in a lease under which the landlord can exercise some control over what the tenant does, subject to a requirement of reasonableness on the part of the landlord, are very familiar, especially in the context of assignment and underletting, and alterations. This is not quite the same, since Colvia, in promulgating the scheme, is acting as management company, not as landlord. Nevertheless, and despite the ownership of the management company by the lessees, it seems to me that cases about assignment or alterations provide a useful analogy."

Analysing the law on assignment, he considered the analysis by Balcome LJ in *International Drilling Fluids Ltd v Louisville Investment (Uxbridge) Ltd* [1986] Ch 513, at 519 to 521, and quoted with approval the statement:

> "But in my judgment a proper reconciliation of those two streams of authority can be achieved by saying that while a landlord need usually only consider his own relevant interests, there may be cases where there is such a disproportion between the benefit to the landlord and the detriment to the tenant if the landlord withholds his consent to an assignment, that it is unreasonable for the landlord to refuse consent."

He then went on to explain that the onus lay on those who assert that the scheme is unreasonable to prove that it is:

> "In order to prove this, it has to be shown that the basis on

> which the decision to promulgate the scheme was founded was not one which a reasonable landlord (or, here, management company) could have adopted in the circumstances."

This exercise, he suggested, had something in common with the familiar public law test of *Wednesbury* unreasonableness.

CHAPTER SEVEN

AFTERWORD

The title of the present work notwithstanding, it will be seen that there is no single set of rules which constitute "the law of parking" in either England or Scotland, let alone the whole of Great Britain. Rather, what there is instead is a patchwork of common law principles, legislative interventions and industry practice including voluntary codes, the applicability of all of which depends not only upon territorial jurisdiction but also subject-matter context.

The answer to the simple question "can I park here?" can be altogether different depending upon whether "here" is a public road, a private road, a council car park, a private car park, or whether the owner of the car park is a member of a relevant trade association, or an independent actor, and whether the person who wants to park is a member of the public, a tenant, or an owner of adjacent land, or whether he has business with the tenant or owner.

Such a patchwork is by no means unusual in the legal systems of Scotland or England where the *zeitgeist* has always favoured incremental development rather than rigid codification, but it certainly leads to an interesting life for lawyers, not to mention those who just want to park their vehicles lawfully.

It is hoped that the present work will at least give some guideposts for those who seek to negotiate this maze.

However, it must always be remembered that we are not dealing with the laws of the Medes and the Persians, which is fixed and immutable, but with a living, developing *corpus juris* which is in a constant process of changing and adapting to meet the changing needs of society.

Thus, the present work can give only a snapshot at a single point in time. Who knows what changes will come?

For example, will the BPA's *Private Sector Single Code of Practice*, be effective in imposing some uniformity in a private parking market where, not so long ago, anything (up to and including wheel-clamping) seemed to go? Will the Government bite the bullet and promulgate the universal statutory code to which the legislation appears to commit them?

In an increasingly green policy environment, will there be an acceleration of the trend, already present, for planning authorities to impose conditions limiting the parking provided in both commercial and residential developments? Will such measures be effective in driving down car ownership and use? Will they force the man on the Clapham Omnibus to leave his comfortable and convenient car and climb back on the bus?

How might such measures affect society's views of what is reasonable, and how far, if at all, might any such changing attitudes be reflected in the continuing development of the common law?

It would be a bold person indeed who would commit to answering these questions; and even if the shape of future changes in parking law seem clear, there should never be discounted the possibility of a black swan swimming onto the scene.

After all, in the year 2000 the Scottish Law Commission confidently asserted:

> "No new servitude has been recognised for 200 years, and the law of servitudes seems to have stopped when the law of real burdens began, in the closing years of the eighteenth century."

Little did they know.

MORE BOOKS BY LAW BRIEF PUBLISHING

A selection of our other titles available now:-

'A Practical Guide to the Independent School Standards – September 2023 Edition' by Sarah McKimm
'A Practical Guide to Estate Administration and Crypto Assets' by Richard Marshall
'A Practical Guide to Managing GDPR Data Subject Access Requests – Second Edition' by Patrick O'Kane
'A Practical Guide to Parental Alienation in Private and Public Law Children Cases' by Sam King QC & Frankie Shama
'Contested Heritage – Removing Art from Land and Historic Buildings' by Richard Harwood QC, Catherine Dobson, David Sawtell
'The Limits of Separate Legal Personality: When Those Running a Company Can Be Held Personally Liable for Losses Caused to Third Parties Outside of the Company' by Dr Mike Wilkinson
'A Practical Guide to Transgender Law' by Robin Moira White & Nicola Newbegin
'A Practical Guide to 'Stranded Spouses' in Family Law' by Mani Singh Basi
'A Practical Guide to Residential Freehold Conveyancing' by Lorraine Richardson
'A Practical Guide to Pensions on Divorce for Lawyers' by Bryan Scant
'A Practical Guide to Challenging Sham Marriage Allegations in Immigration Law' by Priya Solanki
'A Practical Guide to Digital Communications Evidence in Criminal Law' by Sam Willis
'A Practical Guide to Legal Rights in Scotland' by Sarah-Jane Macdonald
'A Practical Guide to New Build Conveyancing' by Paul Sams & Rebecca East
'A Practical Guide to Defending Barristers in Disciplinary Cases' by Marc Beaumont
'A Practical Guide to Inherited Wealth on Divorce' by Hayley Trim
'A Practical Guide to Practice Direction 12J and Domestic Abuse in Private Law Children Proceedings' by Rebecca Cross & Malvika Jaganmohan

'A Practical Guide to Confiscation and Restraint' by Narita Bahra QC, John Carl Townsend, David Winch
'A Practical Guide to the Law of Forests in Scotland' by Philip Buchan
'A Practical Guide to Health and Medical Cases in Immigration Law' by Rebecca Chapman & Miranda Butler
'A Practical Guide to Bad Character Evidence for Criminal Practitioners by Aparna Rao
'A Practical Guide to Extradition Law post-Brexit' by Myles Grandison et al
'A Practical Guide to Hoarding and Mental Health for Housing Lawyers' by Rachel Coyle
'A Practical Guide to Psychiatric Claims in Personal Injury – 2nd Edition' by Liam Ryan
'Stephens on Contractual Indemnities' by Richard Stephens
'A Practical Guide to the EU Succession Regulation' by Richard Frimston
'A Practical Guide to Solicitor and Client Costs – 2nd Edition' by Robin Dunne
'Constructive Dismissal – Practice Pointers and Principles' by Benjimin Burgher
'A Practical Guide to Religion and Belief Discrimination Claims in the Workplace' by Kashif Ali
'A Practical Guide to the Law of Medical Treatment Decisions' by Ben Troke
'Fundamental Dishonesty and QOCS in Personal Injury Proceedings: Law and Practice' by Jake Rowley
'A Practical Guide to the Law in Relation to School Exclusions' by Charlotte Hadfield & Alice de Coverley
'A Practical Guide to Divorce for the Silver Separators' by Karin Walker
'The Right to be Forgotten – The Law and Practical Issues' by Melissa Stock
'A Practical Guide to Planning Law and Rights of Way in National Parks, the Broads and AONBs' by James Maurici QC, James Neill et al
'A Practical Guide to Election Law' by Tom Tabori
'A Practical Guide to the Law in Relation to Surrogacy' by Andrew Powell
'A Practical Guide to Claims Arising from Fatal Accidents – 2nd Edition' by James Patience
'A Practical Guide to the Ownership of Employee Inventions – From Entitlement to Compensation' by James Tumbridge & Ashley Roughton
'A Practical Guide to Asbestos Claims' by Jonathan Owen & Gareth McAloon

'A Practical Guide to Stamp Duty Land Tax in England and Northern Ireland' by Suzanne O'Hara
'A Practical Guide to the Law of Farming Partnerships' by Philip Whitcomb
'Covid-19, Homeworking and the Law – The Essential Guide to Employment and GDPR Issues' by Forbes Solicitors
'Covid-19 and Criminal Law – The Essential Guide' by Ramya Nagesh
'Covid-19 and Family Law in England and Wales – The Essential Guide' by Safda Mahmood
'A Practical Guide to the Law of Unlawful Eviction and Harassment – 2nd Edition' by Stephanie Lovegrove
'Covid-19, Brexit and the Law of Commercial Leases – The Essential Guide' by Mark Shelton
'A Practical Guide to Costs in Personal Injury Claims – 2nd Edition' by Matthew Hoe
'A Practical Guide to the General Data Protection Regulation (GDPR) – 2nd Edition' by Keith Markham
'Ellis on Credit Hire – Sixth Edition' by Aidan Ellis & Tim Kevan
'A Practical Guide to Working with Litigants in Person and McKenzie Friends in Family Cases' by Stuart Barlow
'Protecting Unregistered Brands: A Practical Guide to the Law of Passing Off' by Lorna Brazell
'A Practical Guide to Secondary Liability and Joint Enterprise Post-Jogee' by Joanne Cecil & James Mehigan
'A Practical Guide to the Pre-Action RTA Claims Protocol for Personal Injury Lawyers' by Antonia Ford
'A Practical Guide to Neighbour Disputes and the Law' by Alexander Walsh
'A Practical Guide to Forfeiture of Leases' by Mark Shelton
'A Practical Guide to Coercive Control for Legal Practitioners and Victims' by Rachel Horman
'A Practical Guide to the Law of Driverless Cars – Second Edition' by Alex Glassbrook, Emma Northey & Scarlett Milligan
'A Practical Guide to TOLATA Claims' by Greg Williams
'A Practical Guide to Elderly Law – 2nd Edition' by Justin Patten
'A Practical Guide to Responding to Housing Disrepair and Unfitness Claims' by Iain Wightwick

'A Practical Guide to the Law of Bullying and Harassment in the Workplace' by Philip Hyland
'How to Be a Freelance Solicitor: A Practical Guide to the SRA-Regulated Freelance Solicitor Model' by Paul Bennett
'A Practical Guide to Prison Injury Claims' by Malcolm Johnson
'A Practical Guide to the Small Claims Track – 2nd Edition' by Dominic Bright
'A Practical Guide to Advising Clients at the Police Station' by Colin Stephen McKeown-Beaumont
'A Practical Guide to Antisocial Behaviour Injunctions' by Iain Wightwick
'Practical Mediation: A Guide for Mediators, Advocates, Advisers, Lawyers, and Students in Civil, Commercial, Business, Property, Workplace, and Employment Cases' by Jonathan Dingle with John Sephton
'The Mini-Pupillage Workbook' by David Boyle
'A Practical Guide to Crofting Law' by Brian Inkster
'A Practical Guide to the Law of Domain Names and Cybersquatting' by Andrew Clemson
'A Practical Guide to the Law of Gender Pay Gap Reporting' by Harini Iyengar
'NHS Whistleblowing and the Law' by Joseph England
'Employment Law and the Gig Economy' by Nigel Mackay & Annie Powell
'A Practical Guide to Noise Induced Hearing Loss (NIHL) Claims' by Andrew Mckie, Ian Skeate, Gareth McAloon
'An Introduction to Beauty Negligence Claims – A Practical Guide for the Personal Injury Practitioner' by Greg Almond
'Intercompany Agreements for Transfer Pricing Compliance' by Paul Sutton
'Zen and the Art of Mediation' by Martin Plowman
'A Practical Guide to the SRA Principles, Individual and Law Firm Codes of Conduct 2019 – What Every Law Firm Needs to Know' by Paul Bennett
'A Practical Guide to Adoption for Family Lawyers' by Graham Pegg
'A Practical Guide to Industrial Disease Claims' by Andrew Mckie & Ian Skeate
'A Practical Guide to Conducting a Sheriff Court Proof' by Andrew Stevenson
'A Practical Guide to Vicarious Liability' by Mariel Irvine
'A Practical Guide to Applications for Landlord's Consent and Variation of Leases' by Mark Shelton
'A Practical Guide to Relief from Sanctions Post-Mitchell and Denton' by Peter Causton

'A Practical Guide to Equity Release for Advisors' by Paul Sams
'A Practical Guide to Financial Services Claims' by Chris Hegarty
'The Law of Houses in Multiple Occupation: A Practical Guide to HMO Proceedings' by Julian Hunt
'Occupiers, Highways and Defective Premises Claims: A Practical Guide Post-Jackson – 2nd Edition' by Andrew Mckie
'A Practical Guide to Financial Ombudsman Service Claims' by Adam Temple & Robert Scrivenor
'A Practical Guide to Running Housing Disrepair and Cavity Wall Claims: 2nd Edition' by Andrew Mckie & Ian Skeate
'A Practical Guide to Holiday Sickness Claims – 2nd Edition' by Andrew Mckie & Ian Skeate
'Arguments and Tactics for Personal Injury and Clinical Negligence Claims' by Dorian Williams
'A Practical Guide to Drone Law' by Rufus Ballaster, Andrew Firman, Eleanor Clot
'A Practical Guide to Compliance for Personal Injury Firms Working With Claims Management Companies' by Paul Bennett
'RTA Allegations of Fraud in a Post-Jackson Era: The Handbook – 2nd Edition' by Andrew Mckie
'RTA Personal Injury Claims: A Practical Guide Post-Jackson' by Andrew Mckie
'On Experts: CPR35 for Lawyers and Experts' by David Boyle
'An Introduction to Personal Injury Law' by David Boyle

These books and more are available to order online direct from the publisher at www.lawbriefpublishing.com, where you can also read free sample chapters. For any queries, contact us on 0844 587 2383 or mail@lawbriefpublishing.com.

Our books are also usually in stock at www.amazon.co.uk with free next day delivery for Prime members, and at good legal bookshops such as Wildy & Sons.

We are regularly launching new books in our series of practical day-to-day practitioners' guides. Visit our website and join our free newsletter to be kept informed and to receive special offers, free chapters, etc.

You can also follow us on Twitter at www.twitter.com/lawbriefpub.